IN THE HOUR
OF THE WOLF
TALES OF A SÁMI WARRIOR

NIILLAS SOMBY

Edited by Gabriel Kuhn

PM

In the Hour of the Wolf: Tales of a Sámi Warrior
© 2026 Niillas Somby
This edition © 2026 PM Press

ISBN: 979-8-88744-176-4 (paperback)
ISBN: 979-8-88744-177-1 (ebook)
Library of Congress Control Number: 2025943638

Translation by Margarita Emelianova
Cover design by John Yates / stealworks.com
Interior design by briandesign
All images courtesy of Niillas Somby

This translation has been published with the financial support of NORLA.

NORLA
Norwegian
Literature Abroad

10 9 8 7 6 5 4 3 2 1

PM Press
PO Box 23912
Oakland, CA 94623
www.pmpress.org

Printed in the USA.

Praise for *In the Hour of the Wolf*

"*In the Hour of the Wolf* by Niillas Somby documents an important moment in the anticolonial struggle of the Sámi people of northern Europe. In 1982 Somby was badly injured, losing an arm and an eye while attempting to sabotage construction of a hydroelectric dam on the Álta River in Norway. Imprisoned for the sabotage attempt, Somby was able to escape and made his way to Canada, where he found shelter with Indigenous peoples, including George Manuel of the Secwepemc nation, until his charges in Norway were dropped. *In the Hour of the Wolf* provides a fascinating account of the Sámi people's struggles and the life of Niillas Somby."
—Gord Hill, Kwakwaka'wakw, author of *500 Years of Indigenous Resistance* and *The 500 Years of Indigenous Resistance Comic Book*

"This is an important book, in which Niillas Somby traces the lines from the resistance against the development of the Álta River to the Sámi Parliament and the institutionalization of Sámi rights."
—Samisk bibliotektjeneste, Sámi Library Services

"The book provides personal insight on a resistance movement that has met little recognition while having been crucial in the struggle for Sámi rights."
—Tina Andersen Vågenes, Anarres

"*In the Hour of the Wolf* is an important book that presents voices which have long been silenced."
—Ivar Bjørklund, *Nordnorsk debatt*

PREFACE

Gabriel Kuhn

Niillas Somby is an icon of the Sámi resistance movement. In 1982, he lost an arm and an eye during a failed attempt to damage a bridge leading to a hydropower dam construction site. The action was part of the struggle against development plans along the Áltá River, a pivotal moment in the history of the Sámi standing up for their rights as the Indigenous people of northern Europe. Facing a long prison term, Somby managed to escape to Canada where he was adopted and sheltered by First Nations until the main charges against him were dropped and it was safe for him and his family to return to Norway.

In the Hour of the Wolf is Niillas Somby's own account of these tumultuous years. They provide an insight into the Sámi resistance movement, transnational Indigenous solidarity, and the reality of First Nations in Canada in the 1980s. Somby adds important political reflections.

"Hour of the wolf" is a common phrase in the Nordic countries, popularized by the 1968 Ingmar Bergman film of the same name. In it, the phrase is introduced as follows: "The hour of the wolf is the hour between night and dawn. It is the hour when most people die, when sleep is deepest, when nightmares are most real. It is the hour when the sleepless are haunted by their greatest dread, when ghosts and demons most powerful. The hour of the wolf is also the hour when most children are born."

I got to know Niillas in 2019, while working on the book *Liberating Sápmi: Indigenous Resistance in Europe's Far North*. We met in his hometown of Deanušaldi, and I was treated to a fascinating three-hour synopsis of this book. The original Sámi edition, *Gumppe diimmus*, was already out, published in 2016. In 2022, the Norwegian edition followed, titled *I ulvens time*. I feel very honored that Niillas entrusted me with the editorial work on the English edition you are holding in your hands.

My main task was to edit an English draft of the book handed to me by Niillas's partner, Margarita Emelianova. In consultation with the publishers at PM Press, I also added this preface as well as explanatory notes. Not all readers may be familiar with the historical context in which Niillas's story unfolded. Brian Layng, the book's designer, created the maps included.

The Sámi: Origins, Colonization, the Guovdageaidnu Rebellion

The Sámi are the Indigenous people of northern Europe. *Sámi* is the preferred term of self-identification and commonly used since the 1980s, replacing terms that, today, are considered offensive. The term *Sápmi* describes the traditional homeland of the Sámi people as well as the totality of Sámi culture, life, and spirituality. The traditional homeland isn't clearly defined, as the Sámi never laid claim to any territory in a legal sense; the boundaries roughly correspond to the area of prolonged Sámi settlement.

The origins of the Sámi people are unclear, but scholars agree that they arrived in the region known as Fennoscandia roughly around 2000 BC coming from the east. Fennoscandia signifies the large peninsula encompassing Scandinavia, Finland, Karelia, and the Kola Peninsula in today's Russia.

In the course of the centuries, the Sámi settled along the northern coast of modern-day Norway and went farther south. Archaeological excavations have revealed a Sámi presence at around 1000 BC in the Swedish province of Härjedalen, located on the border to Norway, a mere four hundred kilometers north of Oslo.

In line with anthropological studies of nomads as "societies without a state," traditional Sámi society has been described as "anarchist."* It consisted of roaming groups of about a hundred people. North Americans are often surprised about the striking parallels to Native American cultures, which include religious and artistic practices as well as material objects of everyday use such as shamanic drums and tipi-like tents. As nomads in the Arctic region, the Sámi are considered the inventors of the ski, used as means of transport thousands of years ago.

For survival, the Sámi mainly relied on hunting and fishing. Reindeer were domesticated and used as working animals early on, but only in the sixteenth century did large-scale breeding and herding begin. While the majority of Sámi never owned reindeer and less than 10 percent of the Sámi population is involved in reindeer herding today, the reindeer are highly significant for Sámi identity, culture, and mythology.

The Sámi started trading hides and handicrafts with outsiders during the Viking Age (793-1066) but remained largely independent before the Swedish government (which, at the time, controlled both modern-day Norway and Finland) implemented policies to settle the north in the seventeenth century. This was in no small part related to the opening of a silver mine near Árjepluovve. The Swedish

---

* Christian Mériot, *Samerna* (Furulund: Alhambra, 1994), 4.

government understood that money was to be made in the north, and it encouraged settlers to move there, exempting them from taxes and offering them land that had been used by Sámi hunters, fishers, and reindeer herders for centuries. Sámi were used as forced laborers and coolies. Resistance was met with harsh repression.

What followed was a period of colonization all too familiar from territories conquered by European powers across the world. The Sámi were forced to relocate, their cultural and spiritual traditions were outlawed, they were Christianized under threat (dozens of *noaidi*, "shamans," were burned at the stake), and their children were gathered in boarding schools adhering to strict assimilation policies: speaking the Sámi language was not allowed, and children were often only allowed to see their families at Christmas and over the summer.

The Sámi were also subjected to anatomical studies and medical experiments, mainly at the hands of the State Institute for Racial Biology, established at Sweden's most prestigious university, Uppsala, in 1922. Meanwhile, both artefacts and human remains were shipped to research facilities and museums.

The state took control of the forests and the waterways and began to extract minerals. It drew national borders across Sápmi that divided families, cut off pastures, and introduced bureaucracy alien to Sámi culture. In the 2016 Swedish TV series *Midnight Sun*, one of the first to feature Sámi culture in a more nuanced manner, a Swedish helicopter pilot explains to a French visitor: "They've taken everything from the Sámi except for reindeer herding—probably because it is such hard work." In 2004, Victoria Harnesk of the Sámi Association in Stockholm stated: "We, the Sámi people, have not been subject to a bloody genocide but of a cultural, 'soft' genocide, based on hidden but effective tools employed by the Swedish state to steal our land, water, language, religion, identity, and the possibility to pursue our traditional livelihoods."[*]

The first open Sámi rebellion against colonization arose from Læstadianism, a Pietist Sámi-Christian revival movement. Læstadianism is named after its founding figure, the priest Lars Levi Læstadius, who, in the 1830s, used Sámi mythology to reach a Sámi audience, while at the same time turning his followers against central aspects of Sámi culture such as the yoik, traditional Sámi singing. Læstadius's promise was to escape the hardship the Sámi were experiencing through adherence to a strict moral, which convinced a significant number of Sámi who felt that their culture's foundation was crumbling under colonization. This led to the Guovdageaidnu Rebellion of 1852, in which a group of about fifty Sámi descended on the town of the same name (a center of Sámi culture to this day) and killed a government official and a merchant, before being overwhelmed by local residents. Two alleged ringleaders, Aslak Jacobsen Hætta and Mons Aslaksen Somby, were executed—the latter being one of Niillas Somby's ancestors. In 1999, the documentary film *Give Us Our Skeletons!* chronicled Niillas's efforts to have Mons Aslaksen Somby's remains returned to Sápmi.

The Guovdageaidnu Rebellion is a unique event in Sámi history, as Sámi resistance is otherwise marked by a near complete absence of violence. The renowned Sámi poet Nils-Aslak Valkeapää liked to emphasize that there was no word for "war" in the Sámi language.

---

[*] Victoria Harnesk, "You Have to Be Visible—to Exist?," open letter to Swedish Prime Minister Göran Persson and UN Secretary General Kofi Annan regarding the Stockholm International Forum Conference on the Holocaust, January 25, 2004. Quoted from www.klevius.info/genocide-1.pdf. Edited for consistency in spellings.

Political Organization

The political organization of the Sámi began in the early twentieth century. Elsa Laula, born in Dearna in 1877, emerged as a prominent leader. She was the driving force behind one of the first Sámi organizations, Sweden's Lapparnas Centralförbund (Central Association of Lapps/Sámi), founded in 1904. Laula envisioned a pan-Sámi movement reaching beyond colonial borders. In her 1904 treatise *Inför lif eller död* (Facing Life or Death), she wrote: "The Lapps need to take things into their own hands. 'In what way?' many ask. There is only one: to build a united Lapp association that plants roots everywhere within the Lapp population…. To you, young men and women, I will say one thing: the future of our people lies in your hands! With your strength, our people and our land shall persevere."*

In 1917, Laula organized the first Sámi National Assembly in Troandin. The date of the meeting, February 6, is today celebrated as the Sámi's official national day. Elsa Laula's portrait is ever-present in Sápmi, adorning artwork, posters, and graffitied walls.

After World War II, national Sámi organizations such as Samii Litto (Sámi Union) in Finland, Norske Reindriftsamers Landsforbund (National Association of Reindeer-Herding Sámi in Norway), and Svenska Samernas Riksförbund (National Association of Sámi in Sweden) were founded. Of particular importance was the foundation of the Sámi Council in 1956, which brought together Sámi organizations from Norway, Sweden, and Finland.** In 1992, Sámi representatives from Russia also joined.

---

* Elsa Laula, *Inför lif eller död* (Stockholm: Wilhelmssons, 1904), 27-29. Translated by G.K.
** The English spelling traditionally used is "Saami Council." Here, it has been adapted to the spellings used in this book.

The Áltá Conflict

The so-called Áltá Conflict from 1979 to 1982 is often referred to as the starting point of the "Sámi civil rights movement." Questions of terminology aside, it was without doubt a decisive moment for the formation of contemporary Sámi resistance against the ongoing colonization of their homeland.

When, in 1968, the Norwegian government presented plans for building a hydroelectric power dam along the Áltá-Guovdageaidnu River, the plans were met with much resistance both by Sámi and environmentalist groups. Hydropower was a highly charged issue since numerous hydropower stations had already been built in Sápmi following World War II, including thirteen along the Lule River alone, which runs through Sápmi's heartland. The dams made large areas of land unsuitable for reindeer herding and interfered with waterways that were essential for the Sámi both as freshwater sources, fishing grounds, and travel routes.

While protests around the Áltá-Guovdageaidnu hydropower plans had to be expected, the strength and the breadth of the resistance movement caught most by surprise. The access to the construction site was blockaded for months and the protests received much international attention—Winona LaDuke and Julie Felix organized solidarity campaigns in North America.

Eventually, a group of Sámi decided to take the resistance to the Norwegian capital Oslo, about one thousand miles south of Áltá. On October 8, 1979, they erected a traditional Sámi dwelling outside of the parliament building, and about ten of them went on hunger strike, Niillas Somby included.* The strike ended a week later, when prime

---

* The exact number is disputed. See Niillas's account.

minister Odvar Nordli promised to hold construction along
the Áltá-Guovdageaidnu River while parliament was to
investigate the matter anew.

Without significant changes to its outline, however,
work on the Áltá-Guovdageaidnu dam was to resume in late
1980. When the protest camp along the access road to the
construction site at Nullpunktet (Ground Zero) was reestab-
lished, six hundred police were sent to Áltá on a passenger
ferry. They cleared out the camp on January 14, arresting
nine hundred people and deporting a number of Sámi from
Sweden and Finland, which was a huge offense to pan-Sámi
identity.

The Sámi's last hope was that the courts would rule in
their favor. But on February 26, 1982, the Supreme Court
of Norway upheld the government's decision to build the
dam. The Sámi's means of resistance had seemingly come
to an end.

But not everyone accepted defeat, Niillas Somby among
them. On March 20, 1982, he and two companions attempted
to damage a bridge leading to the Áltá-Guovdageaidnu dam
construction site. How this unfolded and the series of events
triggered by it are the subject of this book.

The Áltá-Guovdageaidnu dam opened in 1987.
Decades later, the Norwegian government conceded that
it had boosted energy production in Sápmi much less than
predicted.

Áltá: The Consequences

Despite the eventual construction of the Áltá-Guovdageaidnu
dam, the Áltá protests are generally regarded as a success.
They put Sápmi on the map and caused unprecedented
media interest in the plight of northern Europe's Indigenous
people. A people that, in the eyes of mainstream society, had

largely been invisible or even nonexistent, had emerged as a self-confident player on the political scene. As historian Björn Forseth put it, "The battle over the Álta River was lost, but the war was won."[*]

The momentum and self-confidence gathered by the Sámi resistance movement during the years of the Álta struggle wasn't lost. In 1986, an official Sámi anthem and flag were adopted. In 1992, the Sámi Conference declared February 6 to be Sámi National Day, in commemoration of the 1917 Sámi National Assembly in Troandin.

There were also changes on the political terrain. A Sámi parliament was established in Norway in 1989 and in Sweden in 1993. (In Finland, a Sámi parliament had already been established in 1973.) To this day, however, none of their decisions are binding. While the parliaments have an important representative function and serve as an arena for internal discussion, they have no political power. Legislation over Sápmi remains in the hands of the Nordic nation-state governments. While there have been significant changes in the cultural realm (largely increased budgets for Sámi media, arts, and educational institutions), the lack of progress in the material realm (land rights, economic independence, political sovereignty) has led to increasing frustration, not least among a new, angry generation of Sámi activists.

Norway
Norway is home to the majority of the Sámi people. Exact numbers are hard to come by, as the Nordic countries do not gather data based on ethnicity or race. Self-identification is key. A 2011 United Nations report on the Sámi gave the following numbers: "The Sami population is estimated to

---

[*] Björn Forseth, *Samelands historia* (Solna: Ekelunds förlag, 2000), 270.

be between 70,000 and 100,000, with about 40,000-60,000 in Norway, about 15,000-20,000 in Sweden, about 9,000 in Finland and about 2,000 in Russia."* The Nordic governments cite similar numbers. (A sizable Sámi community also exists in North America, composed of descendants of both migrant laborers and reindeer herders who introduced reindeer herding to Alaska in the late 1890s.)

Niillas Somby grew up on the "Norwegian side" of Sápmi, as it is called in the Nordic languages (the wording has been adopted in the translation of *In the Hour of the Wolf*). It is therefore not surprising that his account focuses on the situation and the politics of the Sámi in Norway. Yet much of what he observes applies to Sweden and Finland as well, even if the national borders do of course impact the Sámi communities on all sides of them.

Another rhetorical aspect of Somby's account should be explained: even if the Sámi are citizens of the Nordic countries, it is common for them to speak of "Norwegians," "Swedes," and "Finns" as others, that is, as members of a culture that is distinct from their own.

Language

Linguists divide the Sámi language into a dozen dialects, of which North Sámi is the one spoken by the majority. This is the dialect that *In the Hour of the Wolf* was originally written in.

In the English translation, all place names are rendered in Sámi, using North Sámi spelling. Following the maps

---

* United Nations Human Rights Council, *Report of the Special Rapporteur on the Rights of Indigenous Peoples, James Arraya, Addendum: The Situation of the Sami People in Sápmi Region of Norway, Sweden, and Finland* (A/HRC/18/35/Add.2), June 6, 2011, 4.

below, you will find a list with the often better known Norwegian, Swedish, and Finnish names.

On a final note, since different Sámi dialects use different spelling, readers might find personal names spelled differently in other texts or documents.

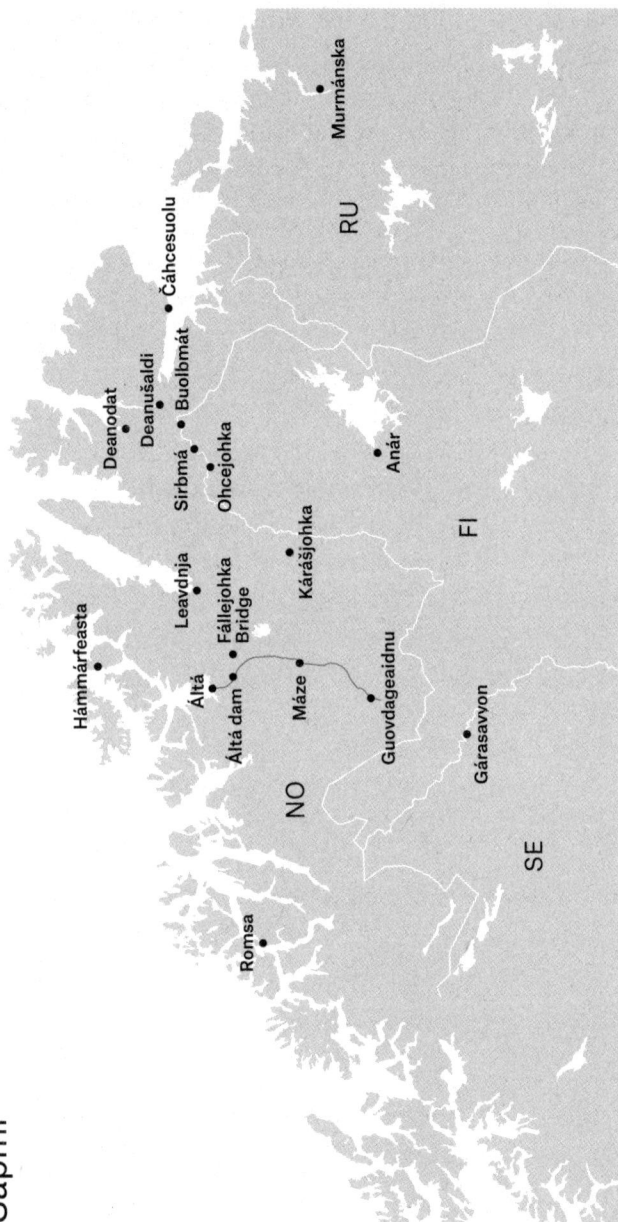

Sápmi

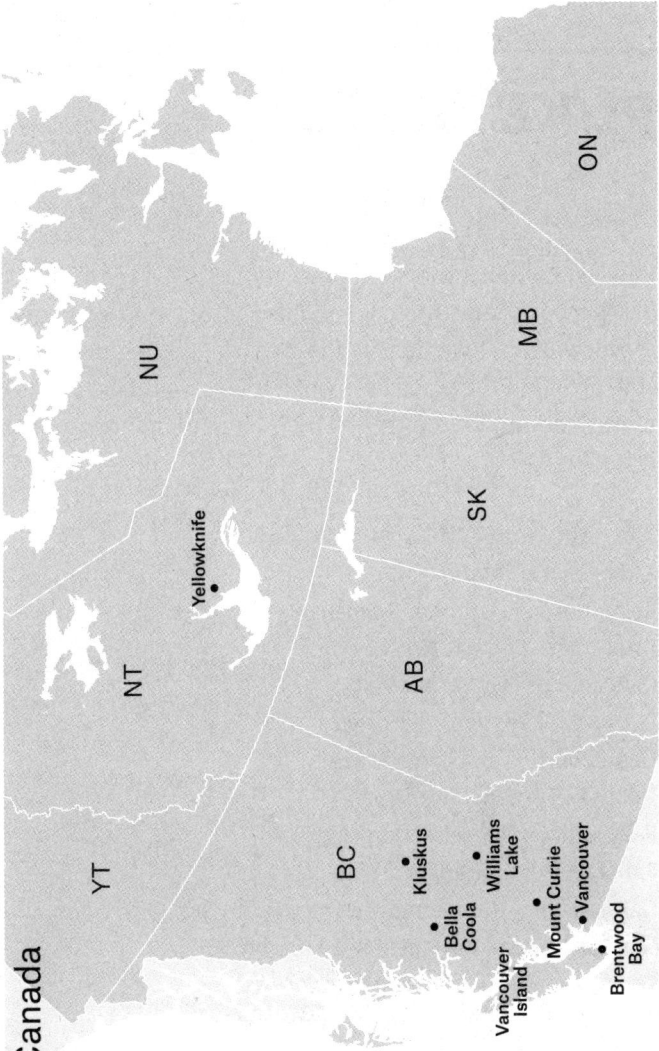

Western Canada

YT

NT

NU

Yellowknife

BC

AB

SK

MB

ON

Kluskus

Williams
Lake

Bella
Coola

Mount Currie

Vancouver

Vancouver
Island

Brentwood
Bay

PLACE NAMES

This list contains the Sámi place names used in this book (in Northern Sámi spelling) and the corresponding names in Norwegian, Swedish, or Finnish, depending on which side of Sápmi the place lies. Small towns, hamlets, or landmarks commonly referred to by their Sámi names are not listed here.

Áltá—Alta *Norway*
Anár—Inari *Finland*
Árjepluovve—Arjeplog *Sweden*
Buolbmát—Polmak *Norway*
Čáhcesuolu—Vadsø *Norway*
Deanodat—Vestertana *Norway*
Deanušaldi—Tana bru *Norway*
Dearna—Tärnaby *Sweden*
Fállejohka—Tverrelvdalen *Norway*
Fanasgieddi—Båteng *Norway*
Gárasavvon—Karesuando/Karesuvanto *Sweden/Finland*
Gáregasnjárga—Karigasniemi *Finland*
Guovdageaidnu—Kautokeino *Norway*
Hámmárfeasta—Hammerfest *Norway*
Horbmá—Horma *Norway*
Johkamohkki—Jokkmokk *Sweden*
Kárášjohka—Karasjok *Norway*
Leavdnja—Lakselv *Norway*
Luleju—Luleå *Sweden*

Máttá-Várjjat–Sør-Varanger *Norway*
Máze–Masi *Norway*
Ohcejohka–Utsjoki *Finland*
Porsáŋggu–Porsanger *Norway*
Rivdul–Riutula *Finland*
Roavvenjárga–Rovaniemi *Finland*
Romsa–Tromsø *Norway*
Sirbmá–Sirma *Norway*
Stuorravuonna–Karlebotn *Norway*
Troandin–Trondheim *Norway*

1.

Two prison guards and two police officers push me into the cell. I sit down on the bed. The large, green iron door makes a thunderous noise when they slam it shut. I hear them lock the door with two different keys. Then they open the hatch and look at me. They close it and lock it as well. I hear their keys jingling as they walk down the hallway of Romsa prison.

I inspect my cell. It's three and a half steps from the bed to the window. Through the bars, I can see rooftops and the tops of birch trees. A brick wall, ten meters high, prevents me from seeing more.

I turn around and walk toward the door. It has a peep-hole hidden by a small inside hatch. I look through it but see nothing. I assume you can only see from the outside in. Then I sit down at the table, on the only chair in the room. The table is as plain as tables get. The only thing on it is a dented red ashtray with the color coming off.

It's early spring but still feels like winter. The year is 1982. While I'm inspecting my cell, there is still some sun on the outside. Too restless to sit still, I walk in circles. It's three steps before I hit the wall, then three steps back. I feel like one of the caged foxes I observed last year at the Buolbmátjávri fox farm.*

---

* Near Buolbmát, on the Norwegian-Finnish border, is a preservation project for the Arctic fox. Buolbmátjávri is the Sámi name for the area's main lake (Pulmankijärvi in Finnish).

I lie down on the bed, wishing I could see the stars. Instead, I stare at a cold concrete ceiling with the one eye I'm still able to use. The ceiling has turned yellow, the result of years of cigarette smoke. I discover graffiti in red ink: "Life is crazy." What did the person mean? Who was he? Why was he here? How many others have been trying to figure out his message? The words are not difficult to relate to. I read them over and over again, thinking about how strange life can be. I remember that, as I was heading for Stilla to protest, I asked my mother for a *peska*, a traditional Sámi coat. My mother is very organized and wastes no time. She headed for the garden shed. From there, I heard her cursing a mouse. As she returned, she put the peska on the table. A mouse had chewed big holes into it. One sleeve was barely hanging on; only a few threads connected it to the rest of the coat. My mother seemed confused. "This is odd," she said. "There has never been a mouse in the shed before." Only today do I understand why the mouse chewed off the sleeve ...

I hear a loud bang. Has the prison been blown up? I try to head for cover, before I realize that it was the same bang I hear all the time—the bang from the Fállejohka Bridge when the bomb went off, tearing off my left hand and leaving me blind in one eye. White bandages are wrapped around my arm, and I still can't believe that my hand is really gone.

John Reier, who is no longer among us, had been not alone in conceiving the action. There was a whole group and we had long discussions. The action had been prepared with care and diligence, both in Áltá and Kárášjohka. Everyone agreed that something had to be done.

2.

John Reier and I took it upon ourselves to carry out the action. We drove on snowmobiles from Sirbmá across the tundra to Giillaš, where the Norwegian Army had a stockpile of weapons. I was carrying a ten-kilo gas cylinder and a cutting torch.

When we got to the stockpile, it seemed easy enough to open the gate. I was trained as an ironworker and had experience from the A/S Sydvaranger mines.* There were only three iron bolts to cut through. They were exposed, so they were easy to reach with the cutting torch.

But, while I was working away, a polystyrene sheet on the inside caught fire. Suddenly, we had a race against time. Would we get the door open before the flames ignited the dynamite?

"Let's get out of here!" John Reier figured we should leave. He was not keen on waiting for the stockpile to explode. But I kept on working on the bolts. I figured that we couldn't give up now. Yet I only ran into more problems. Working on the last bolt, I ran out of gas. I could no longer see much either because of all the smoke. I pulled out my iron saw. Sweating, and with trembling hands, I gave it my best. I was so close!

Finally, the door flew open! We threw as much snow as we could into the arsenal. Some of the plastic that the

---

* A/S Sydvaranger (nowadays Sydvaranger ASA) is a Norwegian iron ore mining company founded in 1906. It operates in the municipality of Mátta-Várjjat.

cartridges and explosives were wrapped in had already melted. At the very last moment we were able to stop the fire. What followed was silence. We heard nothing but the northern winds bending young birch trees. We took a break and had a smoke. The arsenal was in ruins. We took from the king what we needed.[*]

"Here are the stun grenades." I pointed them out to John Reier, but he despised the king and his servants too much to be satisfied with them. He insisted we should take the cartridge boxes as well. "If you use these, you can see them whizzing through the air in the dark!" John Reier also thought that by taking the cartridge boxes, the police would think ordinary thieves had come by. We didn't want them to figure out that someone intended to detonate stun grenades under the Fállejohka Bridge.

We rode back across the tundra in the dark and through heavy snowfall, the booty tied to our snowmobiles. It was hard to find the way under these conditions. The tracks from our approach were already covered in snow. We had to follow our compasses and were relieved when we got a little bit of daylight in the morning—we were heading in the right direction! At Urraoaivi, we hid the booty under a snowdrift, before riding back to Sirbmá.

---

[*] Norway has been a kingdom since 872.

3.

We had a contact in Kárášjohka who had promised to arrange another snowmobile for us. We were supposed to pick it up along the road toward Stilla. Our contact had told us that the snowmobile would have a full tank and a sled. All we had to do was to pull the starter rope and we would be on our way. This man acted like a general, a war hero—yet he was cunning like a fox and made sure he wouldn't get anywhere near the action itself.

When John Reier and I arrived at the agreed-upon spot on the road toward Stilla, we found an old Elan snowmobile that refused to start no matter what we did. We yanked at the starter rope, changed the plugs, cursed, and talked nicely to the old machine, but nothing helped. Eventually, we had to give up and turn around.

We made our way to Áltá, from where we called our man from a public phone. We told him that the snowmobile he had left us was a piece of crap. He denied any wrong-doing on his part but agreed to send people to help. When they arrived, they were mainly busy making phone calls and driving around aimlessly, but they did find a young man who agreed to take us and the explosives to the Fállejohka Bridge. Why he agreed I'm not sure. He looked terrified all the way to the bridge and his voice trembled when he asked us if we really wanted to blow it up. He seemed surprised when we told him that all we wanted was to send a message and that we had no intentions to take down the entire bridge.

"It's just a way of getting attention, of getting the media to write about the Supreme Court ruling we disagree with," explained John Reier.

Some days earlier, the Supreme Court of Norway had approved the government's plans to build the hydropower dam along the Áltá-Guovdageaidnu River. At the stroke of a pen, the Norwegian state had declared our rights as Sámi worthless. Everyone in Sápmi, activists as well as politicians, had anxiously waited for the Supreme Court ruling. We had successfully demanded a halt of all development along the river before the Supreme Court would make its decision.

I had always had a very sober view on politics and no belief in the Supreme Court or any other Norwegian legal institution. Sámi politicians used to laugh at me when I said that these institutions were the Norwegians' institutions, not ours. Yet even for me the Supreme Court ruling was so humiliating that something needed to be done. There was no other way.

Maybe I had trusted the Sámi politicians more than I thought. Maybe their all-important negotiations with the government had made an impression on me, leaving me thinking that, maybe, they might produce results. Otherwise, the Supreme Court ruling would have hardly felt as devastating as it did. Were they simply ignoring our people and our rights? That was hard to take in. Why would any of us have any belief in the Norwegian state left? Perhaps the hard school of Norwegianization that we had gone through had been corrupting than I thought.* Had we bought into the scam of Norway as the world's most democratic country?

---

* "Norwegianization" (*fornorskning*) is a term commonly used to describe the assimilation policies employed by the Norwegian state with regard to the Sámi.

During our first years in school, all we learned was Christian hymns. We knew them all by heart. In history classes, we learned about old Norwegian kings, their battles, and their victories. Meanwhile, our own people were ridiculed, silenced, and made invisible. Our language was erased. Our traditional beliefs were never mentioned by a single word.

Despite it all, we expected some kind of justice from Norway—a country that had tried to wipe us out. Now it seemed obvious that the Supreme Court judges were the same kind as our teachers.

When we arrived at the Fállejohka Bridge, it is pitch dark again and very cold. John Reier and I were very focused. Our young companion stayed in the background; he wanted no part of the crime John Reier and I were about to commit.

I tried to attach wires to an alarm clock. The alarm clock was set to go off at half past four in the morning in order to trigger the stun grenades. We figured that we'd be back in town by then, listening to the morning news about some crazy people who had tried to blow up the bridge. Our man in Kárášjohka was to inform the media. Media attention was the main purpose of our action.

I was still handling the wires with frozen fingers. John Reier tried to help me by shining a half-dead flashlight on the alarm clock. Suddenly, he became very agitated. "The alarm clock has stopped!" He feared that our entire plan would go down the drain. I calmed him down. "Must be the batteries. I have new ones."

Moments later, as I was removing the frozen batteries from the alarm clock, I saw a flash of lightning and heard a thunderous noise as I was thrown a good thirty yards through the air. All I could think was, "Is this how my life is going to end?!"

I was lying on my back in the snow. I was amazed that I could still think even though I was convinced that I was dead. A beautiful creature appeared to my left. She was surrounded by beautiful colors, in the order of a rainbow, radiating peace and love. She had long, glittery hair, and the snow lit up as if the northern lights were shining. The beautiful creature took my hand and looked at me with a warm smile.

"How peaceful it is to die," I thought, wondering why everyone was so afraid of death. I had been, too, but no longer! I was enjoying the moment and had never experienced anything like it.

"Niillas! Niillas! Are you alive?! Are you alive?!" John Reier was panicking. He yanked on my shoulders and shook me really hard, as if he wanted to wake me from the dead.

"I don't know," I said because I didn't know. I tried to move. My feet reacted. I wasn't not sure whether John Reier could see it, but it began to dawn on me that I might not be dead. My left hand, however, I didn't feel—I saw it lying in the snow instead. It was a strange sight. It looked as if was the hand of another person. For a moment, I wondered whether it belonged to the beautiful creature that had stood beside me before John Reier chased her away. I was mad at him for that.

"Niillas isn't dead! Bring the sled, hurry!" John Reier turned to our young companion. Together, they lifted me up on the sled, and John Reier tied a scarf around my elbow to stop the bleeding in the arm that no longer had a hand.

"We will take him to the hospital, they aren't allowed to call the police!" That was wishful thinking of John Reier, but I think he wanted to calm us down, or at least himself. He turned to our companion again: "You can make a run as soon as we get him into a car." The young man was so shaken that he could hardly speak, his face pale enough to shine in the dark.

Riding in the sled of a snowmobile toward Álta at full speed was a living nightmare. The sled dangled all over the place. All I could think of was, "If I'm really not dead yet, I will be soon."

It was a huge relief when the snowmobile stopped. John Reier disconnected the sled, and our companion disappeared, hoping that no one would ever find out that he was with us that night.

4.

John Reier knocked on the door of a nearby house, so hard that I was afraid he would break it. "We had a snowmobile accident," I heard him lie when a man finally opened the door. The man said he couldn't drive us anywhere because he had been drinking. But John Reier wouldn't take no for an answer. "This is a matter of life and death!"

"Then take the car and drive yourself," the man responded. John Reier replied that he would report the man to the police for refusing to help in an emergency. So the man agreed to come with us, but still wanted John Reier to drive. Eventually, with John Reier insisting that he was too shocked to drive, the drunk Norwegian gave in, got behind the wheel, and off we went. Never before had I heard John Reier sing, and I never heard him sing thereafter either. But during that ride with a stranger to the hospital, he was yoiking so loudly that his voice filled up the entire car.* The drunk Norwegian was certainly wondering what he had gotten himself into. Maybe John Reier yoiked so loud to prevent the drunk Norwegian from asking any questions. And, indeed, the only question he asked was: "Are you really sober?"

When we got to the hospital, I told John Reier to leave. "You have to," I whispered. But he insisted on sticking around.

---

* The yoik is a traditional form of Sámi song. See also the preface to this book.

"Mad Sabotage."

"Oh, my God, look at all the burns, and the soot every-where! This can only come from an explosion!" The nurse who first came to see me wasn't to be fooled. She called the doctor right away on the phone. I heard her explain to him that my face was completely black, and that my companion was making up a story about a snowmobile accident. Putting one and one together, she told the doctor straight up that she believed we are protesters who mishandled explosives.

"Get out of here, now!!" One more time, I tried to get John Reier to bail. But he stayed. John Reier had always been stubborn. And I wasn't in a position to do anything about it. He was in charge. I hit him with one more argument: "It'll be easier to handle the police when you're gone." But John Reier still insisted that doctors weren't allowed to call the police.

When the doctor arrived, he cut off my jacket, put bandages around my arm, stuck me with a needle, and put me on a drip. Then, he called the air ambulance to take me to Romsa. Then, he called the cops. John Reier heard it, too, but at that point he had made up his mind. He stayed with me. Now, he was telling anyone around who cared to hear about our action, reminding them they were bound by confidentiality.

5.

At the hospital in Romsa, they concluded that my hand was not to be saved. They put it into a glass of formaldehyde with a name tag on it. The glass they put on a shelf with body parts from the dead. They proceeded to pick debris and gunpowder out of my eye, cutting it up and then sewing it back together. It took them five hours, or at least that's what the doctors told me.

When I woke up from the operation, four policemen in black uniforms with shiny golden buttons were sitting next to my bed. I was thinking that I might have a nightmare again. I closed my eyes. When I opened them again, they were still there.

"We have arrested your friend. We know who he is," said one of the cops.

I didn't like him. "Go to hell," I said.

For some reason, the bed they had put me on was extremely high. It was covered in white sheets. On the radio, they had broken the news about what happened. They had mentioned both John Reier and me by name, and people were sending me bouquets of flowers, which already filled my room. The smell made me sick. An elderly cleaner complained about them, too. Hospital staff had used her bucket as a vase. "We don't have enough of them," a thin Danish nurse said apologetically. That didn't convince the cleaning lady. "Why do people send flowers to a terrorist anyway? Would anyone have cared if this was an ordinary fool?"

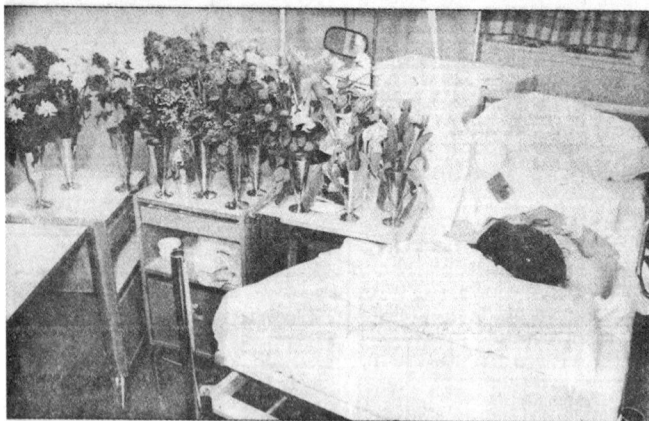

Dagbladet

Løssalgspris 3,50 • Nr. 70 - 114. årg. Onsdag 24. mars 1982

«Superman» ble arrestert i går Side 9

Alta-sabotør ned-dynges av blomster

SAME-AKTIVISTER LOVER NYE AKSJONER

■ ■ Nils A. Somby blir neddynget av blomsterhilsner der han ligger hardt skadd på regionsykehuset i Tromsø. Han blir gjort til martyr etter sprengningsforsøket i helga.

■ ■ Same-aktivister lover nye sabotasje-aksjoner i Alta, også mot demningen og kraftverket som skal bygges.
■ ■ Seinest for et par måneder si-

den ble det blant samer planlagt en sprengningsaksjon mot politiskipet «The Viking». Planen ble skrinlagt for ikke å provosere Høyesterett som satt sammen. **Side 7**

Nils A. Somby har fått brev- og besøksforbud, men blomsterhilsner strømmer nå inn fra fjern og nær til Alta-saboteren. (Foto: Ola Røe)

"Álttá Saboteur Drowned in Flowers."

Getting flowers from people I didn't know was nice, but it also concerned me. The police carefully wrote down the name of everyone sending me things. It bothered me that people who just wanted to be kind ended up in the police files.

I wasn't able to get out of bed by myself and felt terrible, yet the police watched my every move. I was hoping that

★ KLASSEKAMPEN Onsdag 24. mars 1982, nr. 70

FAR TIL NILS SOMBY:

-Galt, men forståelig

— Skal eg seie det eg meiner, så er det litt trist her nå. Det er så det at sabotasje og sprengladninger er farlige greier, men eg er ikkje riktig enig i alt. Det har vore overgrep mot oss samar, og det er ikkje noko nytt, seier Aslak Somby, far til Nils Aslak Somby, til Klassekampen.

— Det er galt det som har skjedd, og det er galt nok om ein ikkje skal bli blind attpå, men eg forstår godt korleis Nils har tenkt og kvifor han har gjort som han gjorde. Ingdomen veit meir enn vi gamle, men vi har da sett ok vi òg, korleis vi t.d. er litt lurte på reintalet vårt g forteneste, seier Aslak omby.

Som så mange andre sam- er han motstandar av byggings av Alta/Kauto-ino-vassdraget.
— Eg har ikkje demon-rert i lenkegjengar og lik-nde, men eg gjekk i fak-ltog, og det er sikkert at

dette er ikkje første gangen det har vore overgrep mot oss samar.

Aslak Somby fortel at ve-ner og kameratar har ringt og vilja dei og kome med god støtte i dei dagane som har gått sidan sprengingsulykka i Alta, men noko familie-besøk til Nils Somby på sju-kehuset blir det ikkje tale om. Kona hans var der like etter at han vart lagt inn, men nå har han forbod mot besøk, såvel som brev, men som Aslak Somby seier:
— Det er galt det som har hendt, men det har vore mange som har trampa over dei samiske interessane òg.

Is Aslak-som Somby var aktivt med under sveltestreiken framfor rtinspd i 1979. Her saman med dei to døtrene sine: Anja (t.v.) på r òr og Sonja på fem år. (Foto: Lars Martin Hjorthol)

"Niillas's Father: 'Crazy, but Understandable.'"

they could smell my farts and wondered if they'd record them for their files, too.

I wasn't doing well. I mourned the loss of my hand and the sight of my eye. Sleep helped me forget, but only on occasion. Mostly, it led to dreams of the explosion, in which I lost both hands and both feet. In those dreams, the police told the doctors which body parts to cut off. When they suggested cutting off my head, I usually woke up.

I wanted to know more about my injuries. I was full of questions, both about my hand and my eye. The nurses didn't dare say much because there was always a cop around. And the police want to ensure that I was not getting any information I wasn't supposed to get.

I was just about to fall asleep when Mads Gilbert, a young doctor, entered. He didn't care about the police and their instructions. He walked up to my bed, held my hand, and introduced himself. He sang the praises of John Reier and me, insisting that we had done the right thing. "Niillas, in the end, everything will turn out all right!"

Never in my life, not before or after, has a person saying hello meant so much to me. I later learned that the hospital's board of directors took disciplinary action against this young, brave man.

6.

I've spent a few days in my cell when I have four visitors from the outside. Two tall, muscular Norwegian men, a skinny Norwegian woman, and a short Sámi with gray hair and a pot belly. They come from the court and want to hold a hearing in my hospital room. The Sámi is acting as a lackey for the Norwegians. As they're settling in, my appointed attorney arrives. He is lanky and bald. The first thing they clarify is that the police need the court's approval if they want to be permanently present in my room. It turns out that the police never bothered to inquire.

I try to make eye contact with the Sámi man. He is from Skiippagurra but now lives in Romsa. I have no luck. He doesn't dare to look at me. His expression never changes, and he speaks only when formally required. He seems like a Sámi who has run errands for Norwegians all his life.

The people from the court make it clear that the police are no longer allowed in my room. They must sit in the hallway. However, they are still allowed to keep all visitors away except close family members. And during their visits, the police are allowed to be in the room with them. The police are also allowed to require everyone to speak Norwegian, so that they understand what's being said. The police are also allowed to accompany the nurses and doctors checking in on me. I, on the other hand, am not allowed to listen to the radio or read the press.

"You must only speak Norwegian!" Dagny is getting clear instructions from the police during her visit. With teary eyes, she is sitting by my bed, holding the hand she can still hold. She is silent but seems happy that I haven't lost that hand, too. We can only meet in silence. How can we speak Norwegian in such an intimate moment, especially when a Norwegian cop is recording every word we say?

The police follow even when the nurses take me to the shower. Eventually, I can go shower myself. One of the first times I do, a young policeman stops me. "What are you doing?!"

"I'm going to have a shower," I say. "Do you want to join?" He doesn't find it funny and asks a nurse if I was indeed allowed to go shower by myself. The nurse has a better sense of humor than him. "Yes. And you should really join him!"

The cop is still not laughing but he does indeed follow me to the shower. When I turn on the water, I pretend to drop the shower head. The cop gets soaked yet acts as if nothing has happened. Only when I spray water on him again and again does he angrily declare that this is against the law.

On the way back to my room, we meet another patient, an old man, who is laughing heartily at the police officer dripping with water from head to toe.

The nightmares about the loss of my hand continue to haunt me. I dream that my bandaged arm is a sick infant that I have given birth to. Sometimes, I tear off the bandages in my sleep, staring at the open wound when I wake up. It feels like I'm looking at Háhcešeatni.[*]

---

[*] In Sámi mythology, Háhcešeatni is a figure representing evil.

One morning, after breakfast, just as I'm about to nod off, I notice a familiar man entering my room. I only catch a glimpse of him behind all the flowers, but I am certain about who he is. I remember what happened last time we met.

I coil up the lasso, cast it, and catch a speckled, unmarked calf. "Daddy, Daddy, come and help!"

My father doesn't have time. He is also catching unmarked calves with his lasso. Right now, he is marking one with yellow-gray fur.

I'm holding on as best I can but get dragged along by the young reindeer. Eventually, I'm able to pull it closer, little by little. The calf is only a few meters away when Daddy steps in to help. Together, we get a hold of it and pin it to the ground. Around us, reindeer herders are competing over who gets to catch the most unmarked calves in the corral. The calves were born last year, we call them vuonjal (females) and varit (males).

I want to mark the calf I caught. My father is holding its head, while I stick the knife into its right ear and carve out our marks: one skivdnji and two bihttá. In the left ear, I carve a njavki and a backwards sárggis.* It takes me time. The competition around us is already over when I'm done.

"Next year, this one will have a calf herself," I say, "so I better put a bell on her." Daddy and I are proud that I have caught an unmarked calf and managed to mark it myself.

"You are a great reindeer-herding Sámi," says my dad and lets the calf go. But it doesn't get very far. A reindeer cop

---

* In order to associate reindeer with their owners, their ears are marked. Each reindeer-herding family has a unique set of marks. Somby uses Sámi names to describe the marks of his family.

grabs it by its horns and shoots it in the forehead.* As the calf is falling to the ground, he stabs it underneath one of its ears. I start crying when I see blood running from the wound. The calf quivers and kicks a few times. Then, it is dead.

"This one we'll take for snacks," says the cop, wiping off his knife and putting it back into the sheath. I am trembling, both of fear and anger.

"What a despicable lowlife," my father says. "But there is nothing we can do."

The man I caught a glimpse of behind the flowers is the reindeer cop. Now he is standing right in front of me. "Niillas, you probably know who I am and why I am here."

Many years have passed since I cried over that calf bleeding to death, but the memory is etched into my mind. It's as if it happened yesterday. Even though I have just lost a hand and an eye and am looking at decades in prison, I am still mourning the calf that this man, a police officer, has taken away from me.

"How did it taste?" I ask.

Sverre Opdal smiles. "I am the one asking the questions."

---

* The reindeer police in Norway (*reinpolitiet*) has existed as a special branch of the Norwegian Police Service since 1949. It is responsible for enforcing the laws regulating reindeer herding in the country. Since reindeer can only be herded by Sámi, it controls, effectively, only the Sámi community.

7.

I am transferred to prison after just one week, wearing ankle chains. So, back to my cell. Apart from the bed, the table, and the chair, there is a sink with hot and cold water.

During the first days there, I was only pacing back and forth. Then, I developed a workout routine using the chair, mainly hopping up and down. I feel that I must exercise, as I have no idea how long they'll keep me here.

I can see a bit of the yard when I look through my window. Once a day, I see prisoners there. They walk in pairs, sometimes in threes. They talk a lot. On occasion, I hear someone sing.

After a week in prison, my father and Dagny come to visit. Visits are supposed to be uplifting, but it's difficult when you can't talk. The rules are the same as they were in hospital: no language is allowed but Norwegian. A prison guard with a tape recorder is sitting next to me. The recorder is switched on as soon as we speak Sámi, and it means that no more visits will be allowed for a long time.

During visits, we are essentially three prisoners in a room with a guard sitting next to us. I can tell that my father is afraid of the guards. But nobody says a word anyway, we just drink coffee and eat the waffles that Dagny has brought. When the visit is over, I give Dagny a hug before I am escorted back to my cell.

I lie down on my bed and, once again, mourn the loss of my hand and my eye. What is going to happen with my life? I am anxious. If I get convicted of the charges they want to try me for, I will spend twenty-one years in prison, and it doesn't look like much can be done to prevent this. My attorney tells me to prepare for the worst. Section 148 of the criminal code, manslaughter and arson, is not to be taken lightly, even if I haven't actually killed anyone or even started a fire.

If I will have to spend twenty-one years in prison, I will be an old man before I'll step out again. The sour smell of nicotine in my cell turns extra sour when I remember what it was like to breathe fresh air. My two little girls, Risten and Anja, will be adults when I get out. And not only that; they will be strangers, too. These thoughts are hard to bear, and I desperately try to get them out of my mind.

I think of things that help me escape my prison cell, such as childhood summers by the sea at Lágesvuotna.*

As usual, I wake up early in the morning, when Father fills the *lávvu* with smoke.** Wet willow trees create a lot of smoke before they turn to embers ...

I get up for coffee and feel ready for breakfast. All we have is smoked meat and dry bread—we have to cut off some mold from the bread before we can eat it. But once we've smoked it and heated it over the embers, we can no longer smell the mold.

Then, Father goes off to look after the reindeer, while my elder sister Alehttá and I stay behind to guard the camp. Old Bolfe barks without end. He is angry because he is not allowed to follow Father to the herd. He only stops barking when we take him to the river. Alehttá has bought a fishing

---

* One of the northernmost fjords in Norway. Laksefjorden in Norwegian.
** A lávvu is a traditional Sámi tent, similar to a tipi.

rod. She is a good fisher and catches one brook trout after another. Bolfe and I hunt mice, and we are both equally excited when we catch one.

"You're not going to be a reindeer herder when you grow up," Father says whenever I don't get a fire going or mess up cutting marrowbones. When I make a hole in a bone, he tears it apart, so that guoržžu, the spirit of misfortune, won't be able to see through it. Every time we finish eating meat soup, Father takes the bones outside. "Run like a reindeer," he says when he throws them onto the ground one by one, always counterclockwise, the same way the reindeer run inside the corral. The marrowbones he places in the creek. There exist odd rules around the camp. Whistling, for example, is not allowed. It attracts strong winds, Father says.

In the fall, I go to school in Deanodat. The first night I have to sleep with twenty other boys in the same room I am terrified. The boys from the coast are used to boarding schools and start snoring as soon as they lie down.* I can't sleep until the sun comes up.

The children from the coast tease and bully me. They call me *badjeáddjá*, an "old reindeer herder." But that doesn't bother me because I love badjeáddjá.

One day, Mrs. Bakke, an old Norwegian teacher, gets angry at an unruly boy, Tor Alf. She puts his index finger into a pencil sharpener, which she twists until blood is running from it. She got angry because the poor lad hadn't been able to memorize a psalm verse. When Mrs. Bakke pulls the boy's bloody finger out of the sharpener, I can no longer stay in the classroom. I run outside, hop on my bicycle, and ride home.

---

* Sámi children living in the more populated coastal areas were easier to force into boarding school than children from remote inland locations. For the significance of boarding schools in Norway's assimilation policies, see the preface.

When it is time to slaughter reindeer, I get a couple of days off school. In the corral, I feel like a man. I follow Father around like a puppy, getting in his way as he tries to catch reindeer with his lasso.

I'm ecstatic when I manage to catch a grown reindeer by myself, even if I get dragged along until some adults step in and hold the rope. I manage to catch a few calves, and Father and I put our marks on them.

When the holidays end, I take the bus back to Deanodat. Mother gets me ready and waits with me at the bus stop. When I see the bus approach, I run away and hide in a cabin built for construction workers. There, I crawl under the table and tie myself to one of the table legs with my belt. The legs are sturdy, as it's a homemade table. I hear mother at the door, she is impatient: "Come on now, the driver is waiting for you!"

It smells of kerosene in the hut. I almost have to throw up. The bus driver arrives with another man. They try to lure me out of my hiding place, while I desperately cling to the table with both hands. Eventually, one of them grabs my feet and starts to pull. "He is strong, that bloody boy!" he says.

I am crying as they try to loosen the belt, which really hurts. I'm just about to give up struggling when I hear Father's voice by the door: "What the hell are you doing? Are you hurting my boy? Go to hell, everyone!" Father is furious and tells the bus driver to leave. I am proud to have such a brave and good father, who chases away the people who are hurting me. When Father comforts me, we forget about school duties. "I need you here. There is a lot of work to do," he says.

I stay at home for a few more days. When I return to school a few days later, our teacher Eva Brustad, the daughter of missionaries, asks me why I have not returned earlier. "There was bad weather on the tundra, and I got lost," I lie.

"Oh, poor Niillas, where did you sleep?"

"I didn't sleep. I just took a nap underneath a large rock."

I always remembered this as a great victory over the school. I don't know what they threatened our parents with, but it was strange that they all obeyed and sent us to school, although for many of us it meant being robbed of our childhood.

I hear the key turn in the door to my cell. A prisoner enters and starts mopping the floor. He is cross-eyed and seems to have a nut loose. He says that he got a one-year sentence for sexually abusing small boys. "The police and the justice system in Norway don't know anything about love," he tells me. "Yes, there is plenty that is wrong with the police and the justice system in Norway," I'm thinking. "For example, how on earth could you only get a sentence of one year?" But I don't tell him that.

When he leaves, I lie down on the bed and have a smoke. I hear prisoners in the yard. A young man laughs as he walks below my window. I inhale and close my eyes. The prisoners in the yard remind me of high school students in detention. My mind takes me twenty-five years back in time, to the winters in Buolbmát, spent in complete darkness.

Everyone rises from their seats when teacher Dybvik comes striding into the classroom like an army officer. He was indeed a commander in the military before he became a school principal in Buolbmát. One year after his arrival, he was elected mayor. He was Norwegian, of course, and a perfect leader for the local chapter of the Labor Party. The Sámi of Buolbmát would have never found such a capable and powerful representative among them.

"Good afternoon, children!" Dybvik's voice is deafening as he walks up to the teacher's desk. It terrifies even the bravest of us. Few dare to look at the great and powerful Norwegian. He grabs a pointer.

"We have reached page 57," he declares, clearing his throat. Then, he looks in his notebook. "Today, Mari will start." He points at Mari, who blushes and begins to read. She stutters a little at first, but she is a good reader, and it is not long before Dybvik stops her with a military-type command. "That was very good," he says in Norwegian, a language that we fourth graders have just begun to understand. During our first years in school, most of us only understood bits and pieces of what the teachers were saying. Mostly, we misunderstood.

"Odd continues," says Dybvik and points at a small boy. We all know that Odd can hardly read, and we expect the worst. Odd's face turns the same color as the red woolen sweater he is wearing. He manages to read a couple of lines, before Dybvik runs out of patience. "Stop, you'll never learn how to read," he says matter-of-factly.

I try to make myself invisible. The thought that Dybvik will ask me to read induces panic. I don't even have the book with me. I left it at home, something I now deeply regret. I have pulled out another book, just so that Dybvik wouldn't notice.

"Niillas continues." I can't utter a word.

"Have you forgotten to wash your ears? Continue reading from where Odd left off!" Dybvik speaks as if he was talking to a deaf person, with his voice growing more and more threatening.

"I ... I ... I forgot the book at home," I finally manage to get out.

"Okay, Kirste continues. Niillas, you will stay here with me after school."

The lesson seems to last forever, but for me it could have continued in all eternity. Much better to sit here with the other children than by myself. And not just because of Dybvik. People say that the school is haunted by ghosts; apparently, a German hanged himself in the attic during the war.[*]

Dybvik checks his watch and closes the book. The lesson is about to finish. We rise from our seats, as we have been trained to do. "Today we sing 'Our God Is a fortress,'" commands Dybvik and gets out the Book of Psalms. Fortunately, Dybvik sings so loudly that none of us could be heard anyway, so I get away with just miming the words.

I'm wondering how I'll get home. Because of detention, I'll be late for the bus, and on top of it, there's a snowstorm outside. Dybvik blares, "Strong as a fortress!"

I remain at my desk, completely still, when the others are leaving. It seems that Britt is glancing at me with pity. Then, I'm alone with Dybvik. He orders me to follow him to his office, which smells of old tobacco. The office has a large desk, a bookcase, and a couple of chairs. There is a portrait of King Haakon VII on the wall in a golden frame. The king's expression is very serious, just like Dybvik's.

"Okay, now you can go home," Dybvik eventually says. "You'll have to walk. I told the bus driver not to wait for you."

The bus usually takes the children first to Hillágurra, Fanasgieddi, and Bildam, about fifteen miles away. After that,

---

[*] During World War II, Norway was occupied by Nazi Germany. Since the far north of the country was of strategic military importance, many German soldiers were stationed there. When the Red Army was approaching in 1944, the Germans applied a scorched-earth policy, burning virtually all dwellings in the northernmost Norwegian province of Finnmark to the ground. The entire population, thousands of Sámi among them, was evacuated, with people returning after the war to rebuild the province, defying government orders.

it's our turn to get home. But today, I might not get home at all. I don't dare to walk past Gáldogurra by myself, as it is known to be a haunted place. Many have seen ghosts there, and I will not walk past it by myself, especially not in the dark.

I try to figure out another way to get home, but I cannot think—my mind is preoccupied by King Haakon. As an adult, I always felt that if I knew where that man was buried, I'd go and piss on his grave.[*]

The police are coming to take me on an excursion. They take me from my cell to a patrol car in ankle chains and put me on the back seat, behind a partition. I light a cigarette.

"Put it out—smoking is not allowed in here!" The cops make it very clear who's in charge.

We are on the way to an orthopedist, who shall design a prosthesis for my hand. My ankle chains are connected by an iron chain to shackles around my arms. Everything is held together by a huge padlock. We are three people in the car, two cops in the front, me in the back.

I pretend not to hear, and the cops yell again: "Put out the cigarette! Now!"

I look at them, take a long drag, and calmly blow the smoke from my nostrils.

"Are you not listening?!" The cops are getting visibly irritated.

One of them turns around, ordering me to put out the cigarette once more: "Smoking is not allowed in the car!"

"Oh, I'm not allowed to smoke in here? I guess that makes me a law breaker. You should arrest me and lock me up!"

"Shut up and put out the cigarette!"

The cop who has turned around didn't find my answer

---

[*] Haakon VII was King of Norway from 1905 to 1957.

very funny, but I think I saw his colleague crack a smile. He doesn't say anything, though, just drives along the icy streets of Romsa.

"Well, if you don't want to arrest me, you can just let me go, that's fine, too," I try.

"You damn Sámi terrorist, you better watch your words!" the angry cop answers.

We stop outside the orthopedist's office and walk in. An old lady sitting quietly in the waiting room becomes distressed when she sees two policemen dragging me along in chains. My right shoulder feels caught in a vise, with the angry policeman grabbing it violently.

There is a no-smoking sign in the waiting room. I decide not to test my luck again. The old lady, who has only one leg, is called to the orthopedist. I sit with the police officers in silence.

"Somby!" It's my turn. A young Norwegian woman is leading us to the orthopedist. She reacts to the angry cop pulling me along violently. His colleague stays in the waiting room. The angry cop tells the woman that he cannot let me out of his sight and needs to listen to every word that's being said. He tells the orthopedist the same. The orthopedist nods and proceeds to address him more often than me. The young Norwegian woman seems embarrassed for the men's behavior.

"Come and get some food!" I'm back in my cell. Outside is a prisoner handing out food to inmates who are not allowed to eat with the others. "Prison is not that bad," I think, as I get a plate and put it on my table. But I don't eat anything. Instead, I put a wet towel over the plate, so that I can't smell the food. Otherwise, I might get tempted to eat something after all. At one point, I remove the towel just for a second to have a look, which I regret immediately. The pork chops look very tempting. I drink some water and feel proud that I didn't give in to temptation. Every time I reject a plate of their food feels like a small victory.

My stomach is aching. I drink some water, while the water pipes squeal badly. I have been without food for almost a week. The hunger gnaws at my soul, and I'm trying not to use too much energy. But I'm determined not to give in. I roll a cigarette and am happy that I can do it myself, thanks to a little red rolling machine that Dagny has brought me. Before that, I had to ask fellow inmates to do it. The cigarette makes me dizzy.

During the hunger strike in Oslo in 1979, everyone said that the hunger strikers shouldn't smoke. But tobacco was our only food and comfort.

There is one thing I ate in prison last week. Oranges. I have not touched anything else, although they continue to bring me food. They have asked several times why I am not eating. "I'm not hungry," was my standard reply. Eventually, they stopped asking me.

One morning, I'm visited by the warden. It's a special event. We start talking about trivial things. Then, he asks: "Why are you not eating, Somby? Is this a hunger strike?"

"It's not a hunger strike," I say. "I just can't eat when I don't feel like it."

I hear someone trying to repair the water pipes. "What are they doing?" I ask. "Will I have to stop drinking the water, too?"

"What do you think, Somby? Do you think we kill people in here?" The warden seems angered by my question.

"I didn't say that. But I'm wondering about something else: what happened to the two fellows who escaped? I assume the cops are good at finding people and returning them."

The warden's face turns red. He gets up and leaves the cell without a word, slamming shut the iron door behind him. I'm left by myself, smiling.

At noon, just as I'm about to take a nap, a prison guard enters my cell with a young Norwegian woman I haven't seen before.

"You have stopped eating," she says and looks me straight in the eye. I decide not to tell her anything before I know who she is.

Not getting a response leaves the woman confused. "Have you started a hunger strike? Are you sick?"

I explain to her that I don't know whether she's a cop or a doctor, and that I've learned that even doctors cooperate with the police. I tell her about what happened at the hospital in Áltá. "So, your promises of confidentiality are not worth the paper they are written on." I also tell her that if she came here as a psychologist, she won't be of much help if she can't speak Sámi. She leaves the cell in tears. The hunger no longer bothers me much, and I feel my plan is working.

The following day, Knut, a relative, visits me. We grew up together. He is now an esteemed doctor in Romsa. He's been sent to speak to me, since the woman yesterday didn't get very far. I trust Knut and tell him about my plan. The plan is that I'll try to convince the prison authorities that I'm worried about them killing me. I want them to believe that I'm not touching their food because I think it might be poisoned. Maybe that gives them second thoughts about trying me under section 148, which would also have an advantage for them, since they wouldn't have to admit that they lied to John Reier and me.

"In that case, you must believe your own lie," says Knut.

He continues to explain that it is not uncommon for a liar to be the first to believe his own lie. "But you must never *completely* believe it. Otherwise, things get out of hand, and you might lose your mind."

Knut suggests for me to claim that I've seen prison guards injecting poison into the oranges they give me. He says that I'll soon be visited by a psychologist called Bjørn Rafter. Knut tells me a little about Rafter and encourages me to stick to my plan and not tell anyone about it.

I'm not sure what Knut said to the prison authorities after he left my cell, but only a short time after his visit, I'm allowed into the yard for the first time to walk around and get fresh air. It feels wonderful to be outside for the first time in weeks, even if I'm surrounded by a brick wall. No other prisoner is in the yard with me.

When I return to my cell, I decide to go into action. I press the button on the intercom: "Can I go take a shower?"

With hot water pouring over me, I finalize my plan. After the shower, I feel ready to fight.

Back in my cell, I throw the two kilos of oranges I have stored on my windowsill into the hallway.

"Are you nuts? What are you doing with the oranges?" The guard on duty is not happy about my actions at all. "Pick it up!"

He lets me out into the hallway. There are oranges everywhere. He is startled, when I scream at the top of my lungs: "I'm sure I'm nuts! And you know all too well why I threw out the oranges!"

I kick one of them, and it makes a huge mess on the wall. The guard throws me back into my cell, where I land on the floor.

I expect other guards to show up, but I see none for the rest of the day. Only a prisoner distributing food shows up.

My stomach hurts again, but I still only drink water. I don't touch the food they bring me. Every time I get a plate, I cover it with a wet towel.

I'm out in the yard again, sitting on the grass, the brick walls around me. It's a warm summer day and I feel the sun on my skin.

Before I stopped eating, I walked a lot in my cell. I managed to do it for hours on end. Now I just sit; my legs no longer have the strength to walk. I'm still allowed to go to the yard, but I'm always by myself. Other prisoners must not talk to me.

A slender Norwegian man appears and sits down next to me. It's Bjørn Rafter, the psychologist Knut was telling me about. Rafter is the head of Åsgård Psychiatric Hospital. He gets straight to the point: "I hear you're worried about being poisoned. I can't tell you whether they want to poison you; I don't know."

I ask him what we can do about it. I say that I've seen prison guards sneak into my cell at night with syringes, injecting something into the oranges. "I was lucky I caught them!" I manage to keep a straight face through it all.

I can tell that Rafter doesn't believe me, but he side-steps the issue. Instead, he invites me to have lunch with him at Åsgård hospital. I tell him that the prison officials will never let me out without chains on my ankles and a cop watching me, and that I don't want to go anywhere under these circumstances. Rafter asks me to wait and goes to talk to the warden. He returns with a smile and says that I can come with me, no chains, no cops.

He takes me to the canteen at Åsgård. It is full of people. Rafter encourages me to take food. "Here, nothing is poisoned!"

It feels good to eat for the first time in three weeks. I must only be careful not to eat too much—a lesson from the hunger strike in 1979.

Rafter and I chat while we eat. Mainly about fishing. We don't talk about prison or poison.

From that day on, Rafter is taking me for lunch at Åsgård every day. My life is getting much easier.

My daughter Risten has sent me two mice made of stone. They have big smiley faces painted on them, and ears and tails added with glue. Tears well up in my eyes whenever I look at them. It's been almost four months since I was able to hold Risten.

One day, I'm visited by two cops. "You have been sentenced to four more weeks on remand while awaiting trial." They want my signature. I have not been allowed to participate in the court proceedings at all. It's not that I'm keen on participating, but I appreciate every opportunity to leave prison.

"You don't need to go through all the details with me. I've heard them before," I say.

I have troubles signing the paper. I cannot use my stump properly yet, and the paper won't keep still on the slippery table. I have to ask the cops to hold it. One of them has a moment of humanity. "How do you feel about the sentence?" he asks.

"I've got used to them," I reply, acting tough.

The court is an arena for those in power to demonstrate their power. The power of the courts and the police is intertwined. The Áltá case has shown this. The authorities had the courts and the police working for them. Therefore, it's no surprise that none of them are showing any leniency now. I'm sentenced to four weeks on remand over and over again. If you're not prepared, it is easy to get disheartened.

VG Lørdag 27. mars 1982 **NYTT** ⑤

Samisk broderring vil bruke våpen:

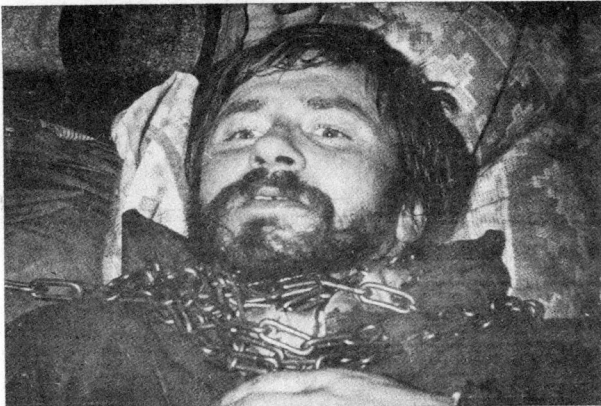

En heltebragd mener medlemmene av den hemmelige broderring blant samer Nils Somby (bildet) utførte da han forsøkte å sprenge broen i stykker. Foto OLAV HASSELKNIPPE

HEMMELIG
aksjonsgruppe

Av ARVE N. AREFJORD

ALTA (VG) — Det finnes en hemmelig samisk broderring på Nordkalotten. Den består av cirka 20 radikale samer med fanatisk tro på at samene nå må ty til våpen for å forsvare seg mot «storsamfunnet».

Innenfor denne klikken blir sprengningsforsøket mot broen over Tverrelva i Stilla for en uke siden sett på som en heltebragd.

De to siktede, Nils Somby og Jon Reier Martinsen, er i deres øyne martyrer. Den harde kjerne av sannsaktivister er knyttet sammen med politiske bånd, men det finnes ingen erklært organisasjon.

Deres mål er at samene må ha enerådenskerett til å råde over det de kaller sannenes eget land, sier en person som har nær tilknytning til det samiske miljø i indre Finnmark, til VG.

Gruppen har et titall medlemmer i Norge. Resten holder til i Sverige og Finland. Aktivistene i Sverige er rekruttert fra vanlige reindriftssamer, mens mange av finnene og nordmennene har akademisk bakgrunn.

Kartlegges

Overvåkingspolitiet har nå flere tjenestemenn i aktivitet for å kartlegge de yterliggående blant disse samene. Etter sprengningsforsøket forrige helg tyder mye på at politiet har rettet søkelyset mot Karasjok. De per ikke bort fra at den omtalte «rødle manne» som må ha vært med under sprengningsraidet, befinner seg der. Innen denne krets av fanatiske samer er nå alle midler legalisert i kampen mot kraftutbyggingen i Finnmark. Nils Somby har uttalt at det var en krigserklæring fra Staten at Høyesterett frikjente Regjeringen i Alta-saken.

Overvåkingspolitiet har nå innhentet en fortegnelse over alle våpen som fremdeles er savnet etter innbrudd og tyverier fra Forsvarets lagre i Finnmark. Overalten av grunn til bekymring. De senere år er antall tyverier økt urovekkende.

Planer

Svenske sannaktivister har angivelig planer klare om sabotasjeaksjoner mot den planlagte kraftutbyggingen i Kalix-elva. På norsk side var det for halvannet år siden konkrete planer om å blåse i luft demningen ved Adamsfjord kraftverk i Finnmark.

Det er umulig å si hvor mange som var innblæret i planleggingen av brosprengningen i Stilla forrige helg.

Politiet mener at det må være involvert minst to personer i tillegg til de siktede. Det kan også se ut som tidspunktet for sprengningen ikke var tilfeldig valgt. Presidenten i Verdensrådet For Urbefolkningar kom i helgen på et lengre ferjevar som planlagt besøk til Finnmark.

Norge er på vakt

Det ble i går ikke registrert nye tilfeller av munn- og klovsyke i Danmark. To dager er gått siden den niende husdyrbesetningen måtte avlives på grunn av epidemien.

Men husdyrsykdommen begynner å sette spor etter i samfunnet. 300—400 danske slakteriarbeidere er permittert nom følge av munn- og klovsykeangrepet.

Veterinærer og bønder her i landet er bedt om å være svært oppmerksomme derson symptomer på sykdommen dukker opp på norske husdyr.

Landbruksdepartementet sendte i går ut ny tidssef om rusttiferen ved den ytterlige sykdommen munn- og klovsyke til alle tollsteder og alle ferjer som får melem Norge og Danmark. På bildet er det veterinæringslister Per Floode som viser plakaten til hun Segerblik.

Først når det står 14 dager uten ny angrep på husdyrene på Fyn, vil danske landbruksmyndigheter gå ut fra at epidemien er på retur.

"Sámi Brotherhood Ready to Use Weapons: Secret Action Group."

"I will read you the charges," says one of the cops. "Even if you no longer want to hear them, it is my duty to do so." He reads from the paper: "You will be charged under section 148 of the criminal code for trying to blow up a bridge. You will also be charged under sections 240, 228-3, and 228-a. Your companion has admitted that the two of you have broken into the Giillaš weapons stockpile to steal cartridges and explosives." One thing has changed, though. They have lifted the ban on listening to the radio and reading the press. It's been about time.

The cops leave, the iron door closes with a rumble, and I'm once again alone with my thoughts.

The cell is three meters long and two meters wide. Three steps forward and three steps back. I wonder how many people have paced back and forth here like this.

I hear prisoners out in the yard. Some stroll by my window. I catch a few words. Young men are laughing. "Kill the Jews!" one of them shouts. I look out the window, trying to get a glimpse of him. "Hey Somby, how are you? Next time you plan to blow something up, let me know, and there'll be nothing left of you!" A tall, skinny Norwegian is looking my way. A guard grabs him by the neck and leads him back inside. "You are not allowed to talk to Somby! Did you forget?"

A short while later, I hear cursing from the cell next door. I can only guess who they've put in there. I take the wooden shoe from underneath my bed and knock three times against the wall. My neighbor answers with four knocks. I'm no longer alone. I have contact with another person, even if it's through a stone wall!

8.

It was difficult to carry out the hunger strike in Oslo in 1979.

The idea was conceived by a group of Sámi in a *goahti* that the late Mihkkal Eira had built at Ground Zero in Áltá.[*]

Mihkkal had built most of the goahti at Ground Zero. In one of them, he lived together with a Danish woman, Ulla. He was one of the people discussing the possibility of a hunger strike.

We had been protesting for a long time and began to understand that Alfred Nilsen, the figurehead of the protest movement, would only talk about Sápmi when he was forced to. We also felt that he and Folkeaksjonen lacked a clear plan for how to stop the construction of the dam.[**] We concluded that we had to take matters into our own hands. Even within the protest movement, we needed to break with the colonial legacy that demanded that Norwegians take the lead, assuming they know better than us.

We could not expect to win in a direct confrontation with those in power. But what is power? Three of us discussed this for a long time: Mihkkal Eira from Máze, Ingar Boine from Kárášjohka, and me.

---

[*] A goahti is a traditional Sámi house, usually pyramid-shaped; it can consist of different material such as peat moss, timber, or fabric. "Ground Zero" (Nullpunktet) was the base camp for the protests against the construction of the Áltá-Guovdageaidnu hydropower dam.

[**] Folkeaksjonen (People's Action) was the main environmentalist organization behind the Áltá protests. While it included Sámi activists, it had a non-Sámi leadership with Alfred Nilsen at its head.

Earlier that year, I had met Kurdish activists at the Indigenous Davvi Šuvva Festival in Gárasavvon, and they had told me about a hunger strike they had carried out in Stockholm.* Mihkkal and Ingar liked the idea, and we started to plan a hunger strike in Oslo outside the parliament building.

Borrowing a small Volkswagen bus from Trygve Lund Guttormsen in Máze, we asked Mihkkal Hætta to serve as a driver. (Neither is with us anymore.) We were heading to Oslo. Our group consisted of Jorunn Eikjok, Mihkkal Anders Gaup, Ingar Boine, and Mihkkal Eira. At Johkamohkki, some Sámi college students joined us: Lars Johannes Svonni, Åke Alla, Sakari Saijets, Hilly Sarre, Bjørg Lifjell, Sissel Lifjell, and Mona Stensgård.** It was important for us to arrive in Oslo with Sámi from all sides of Sápmi. From the Finnish side, we had Bikko Jusse (Jussi Högman) from Ohcejohka. Filmmaker Bredo Greve also joined us with a crew; they traveled in an old Mercedes van, which broke down halfway to Oslo.

We stopped in Troandin, where we told the editors of the newspaper *Adresseavisen* that we were on our way to Oslo to go on hunger strike. The paper published a short article, but it was largely ignored.

In the Dovrefjell mountains, we ran into internal problems, as some of the men had started to drink and smoke on the bus. The college students responded with insults. Jorunn Eikjok demanded the driver to stop and told everyone to get off. She was very determined and made it clear

---

* The five-day 1979 Davvi Šuvva Festival in Gárasavvon brought together Indigenous musicians from around the world. It has at times been referred to as the "Woodstock of the North."

** Johkamohkki is the "Sámi capital" of Sweden and home to numerous Sámi educational institutions.

that there would be no more drinking and smoking on the bus, but that hurling insults was not acceptable either. Everyone got behind Jorunn, and we settled our differences and continued our journey south. No one got any sleep during the journey.

In Oslo, more people joined us: Iŋgor Mihkkala Niillas, Iŋgor Mihkkala Ánde, Nihká Ánde Issát (Isak A. Gaup), the visual artist Synnøve Persen from Porsáŋggu,* and a Sea Sámi from Nord-Troms, Helene Margrete Olsen. We had no clear plans for Oslo beyond going on hunger strike.

When the film crew arrived, we got to stay at Bredo Greve's place. The first few days were chaotic, since we had done no preparation, but people from the Sámi Association in Oslo helped us get organized.** The young people from Johkamohkki soon had enough and left. The ones who stayed painted banners and posters. There was still very little sleep.

After we had agreed on our demands, our South Sámi lawyer, Leif Dunfjell, drafted a letter.

> To the Norwegian Parliament, courtesy of its president, and to the Norwegian Government
>
> Concerning the development plans along the Áltá-Guovdageaidnu River:
>
> The Sámi who are affected by the development plans along the Áltá-Guovdageaidnu River demand that the

---

* Synnøve Persen belonged to an important artist collective, the Máze Group, active in the town of the same name. She went on to have a very successful career as a painter and a poet.

** Many towns in the Nordic countries have their own Sámi associations. "Urban Sámi" are today a significant part of the Sámi population.

issue be brought before the courts. More specifically, we have the following demands:

We demand that the government/parliament stop all further development along the Áltá-Guovdageaidnu River until possible violations of Sámi rights have been investigated by the courts.

We demand a response before Tuesday, October 9, 1979, at 12 pm, about whether the government/parliament will stop the development along the Áltá-Guovdageaidnu River until a court investigation has been carried out.

If we have not received a response by the stated deadline, we will go on hunger strike.

For the Sámi Action Group: Mihkkal Nilsen Eira, Jorunn Eikjok, Niillas Aslaksen Somby

Oslo, October 8, 1979

The letter was delivered to parliament. When we didn't get a response by the stated deadline, we set up a lávvu outside parliament in the way my father had taught me to do.

This time, the Norwegian press was quick to report. Journalists were everywhere, observing and interviewing us all day long. Every word we said ended up in the papers. Foreign journalists appeared as well, and our hunger strike received worldwide attention. We received a lot of international support.

All kinds of people gathered around our lávvu, both passionate sympathizers and fierce opponents. We were supported by a large group of young Norwegians. We knew some of them from Áltá, but here in Oslo, they were also able to bring foreigners with them. Their support was very

The late Mihkkal Anders Gaup, Anders P. Sara, Synnøve Persen, Isak A. Gaup, Nils M. Gaup, myself, the late Mihkkal Eira, and the late Åke Allas.

important for us. They protected the campsite and kept provocateurs and drunkards away; they often came to bother us when the pubs closed.

During the first few nights, we got some sleep in the lávvu. During daytime, sleep was impossible, since the lávvu was crowded by people asking questions about Sápmi. Some know absolutely nothing, and we answered the same questions over and over again.

"How many reindeer do you have?"

"Isn't it cold to live in a lávvu in the winter?"

"Do you pay road taxes?"

"Why do you have such nice, colorful clothes? Do you sew them yourselves?"

There were, of course, more serious questions, too. We answered all of them patiently. Sometimes, we were asked silly questions by people who tried to provoke us, but they

The yoik was heard around the clock in Oslo, and there was never a shortage of listeners.

hardly ever succeeded. Usually, they just got frustrated and became aggressive.

At night, the lávvu turned into a cultural center. Famous yoikers such as Piera Balto, the late Áillohaš (Nils-Aslak Valkeapää), and Simona Máhtte (Mattis Hætta), who went on to represent Norway at the Eurovision Song Contest the following year, come around to perform. We were also visited by the famous Indigenous musician Buffy Sainte-Marie, which produced even more media attention.[*] We set up a PA system, and yoik could be heard throughout central Oslo.

I stayed awake for four full days. My body yearned for rest, but I was too tired to sleep. One day, I was asking our Sámi doctor, Egil Utsi, for a sleeping pill, but he refused to give me one since I was on hunger strike. "Sleep will come,"

---

[*] The 2023 debates about Sainte-Marie's claimed Indigenous identity also reached Sápmi, but this was seven years after Niillas Somby wrote his book.

he said. There must have been power in his words, because I soon fell asleep sitting next to him.

When I woke up, I was cold and confused. I didn't understand where I was. I couldn't move and it was completely dark, but I could hear people talking. I wondered if I was dead. I tried to move my fingers and felt relieved when they responded. My back was wet, and I realized that I was lying in a small pool of water. Then, I panicked because I could feel bodies all around me, and I wondered if they were all lifeless corpses. I felt them wherever I put my hands.

I realized that we were covered by a huge tarp. What misfortune had befallen me? I felt I was on the verge of losing my mind and frantically tried to get the tarp off me. "It's fortunate that they haven't put me in a coffin yet," I thought.

As I was trying to lift the tarp, I caught a glimpse of daylight. I moved toward it as fast as I could. It came from one of the tarp's corners. I finally understood what had happened. While I had been asleep, it had started to rain. Other people were sleeping around me, and someone threw a tarp over us. But water gathered underneath my back, which is how I got wet.

We heard rumors from the north. Apparently, not all Sámi were happy with our action. Some supported us, but others called us a disgrace.

The Sámi Council had a meeting on the Swedish side. One of the members from Norway had a message for us: "Stop embarrassing Sápmi! Go home and be ashamed of yourselves."

The leader of the National Alliance of Norwegian Sámi (Norske Samers Riksforbund, NSR) at the time was Ole Henrik Magga. He declared neither support for nor

The Norwegian does not mind Mihkkal, and Mihkkal does not mind the Norwegian.

Máret Sárá was the editor of the *Charta 79* newspaper during the hunger strike.

opposition to our action and avoided the media the best he could.

Mihkkal Eira was very busy while he was in Oslo. Among other things, he visited parliament because he knew some MPs. He reported back to us from the meetings with them. We got most support from Stein Ørnhøy and Hanna Kvanmo from the Socialist Left.* Through them we also got to know things the government didn't want us to know.

Crucial was the support of Sámi who did not go on hunger strike but who did other, arguably more important, work, for example editing the newspaper *Charta 79*.** The driving force in that group was Máret Sárá from Kárášjohka. Tens of thousands of copies of *Charta 79* were distributed during the hunger strike. The newspaper served as a

---

* The Socialist Left Party (Sosialistisk Venstreparti) is a democratic socialist party in Norway founded in 1975. It has had a continuous presence in the Norwegian Parliament since, gathering between 4 and 12 percent of the vote.
** The newspaper was subtitled "Newspaper for Indigenous Issues." The main title referenced the Czechoslovakian civil rights movement Charta 77.

Niillas with a copy of the *Charta 79* newspaper.

IN THE HOUR OF THE WOLF

powerful tool. It allowed us to get our message out, and the Norwegian government couldn't miss it.

Many people deserve to be mentioned here, among them Egil Utsi, Ánde Somby, Eirik Myrhaug, Josef Riser, Ragnhild Nystad, and others. To this day, it is mind-boggling to think how many people were inspired and motivated by the hunger strike and how the action brought all these people together.

Every day, people stopped by the lávvu crying. They told us that they were Sámi but that they had always hidden their identity. We comforted them and told them that this was not their fault. The fault lay with the cruel policies of Norwegianization.

The hunger strike and our lávvu got the city of Oslo boiling. So it was no surprise when the authorities sent the police to take down the camp. I happened to be on a toilet somewhere when the cops arrived, confiscating the lávvu and arresting everyone in its vicinity.

When I returned, I only found a large crowd gathered where the lávvu used to be. Someone put a bullhorn in my hand, and I climbed onto one of the lion statues guarding parliament. I declared that we wouldn't give up the fight and that the hunger strike would continue despite government repression.

One by one, the hunger strikers returned, and we erected a new lávvu. The hunger strike continued. The media always reported that seven Sámi participated in it, but we were actually ten: the late Mihkkal Eira, Jorunn Eikjok, Synnøve Persen, the late Mihkkal Anders Gaup, the late Ánte Gaup, Nils M. Gaup, Ingar Boine, Isak Aslak Gaup, the late Helene Margrete Olsen, and I.

Before long we received a letter from the government stating that development along the Áltá-Guovdageaidnu

When the police confiscated our lávvu, we set up a new one instead.

River would be halted until the courts had investigated possible violations of Sámi rights. Mihkkal read the letter to us. In his opinion, this was the best we could expect. It didn't solve the problem, far from it, but it gave Sámi politicians some leeway. Perhaps they would be able to stop the natural destruction of our homeland. On October 15, 1979, Odvar Nordli, Norway's prime minister at the time, promised: "For me and for the government, one question is crucial for the assessment of this matter: the Sámi must feel that reasonable time and attention is given to protecting their rights."

In October 1980, the Sámi Rights Committee was formed. It took seventeen years for it to publish a report on Áltá. Halfway through that period, the Sámi Parliament was established. King Olav V opened its first session on October 9, 1989. Not everyone is happy with how the Sámi Parliament operates, but it has brought many jobs; they are also steadier than the ones that came with the construction of the Áltá-Guovdageaidnu River dam.

My reflections on Sámi politics are violently disrupted when I hear banging on the wall of my prison cell. It comes from the cell next to me. I put out the cigarette I'm smoking and throw it in the ashtray. Meanwhile, the ashtray in the neighboring cell seems to shatter into a thousand pieces. That tall, skinny Norwegian boy they put in there is screaming and cursing. He doesn't stop until a guard enters the cell. Maybe they'll take him to the shower to cool off, or they'll let him watch TV. I don't know, and I don't care. I only hope he will be quiet now.

The less food you have in your body, the clearer your mind becomes. Hunger makes your mind wander and reminisce. You search for answers and try to solve the riddles of life. It's dark outside, and all I can hear are the water pipes squealing when someone turns on a tap. I have been up most nights lately and snooze during the day. I stand by the window for some time, which is ajar. It is nice to catch some clean summer air. In the yard, I see seagulls walking on the grass. They have young ones who have started to chirp. Nature is waking up.

Since they lifted some of my restrictions, I now have a radio in my cell. It is a good companion. When I've been up all night, I wait for the morning news in Sámi and inevitably fall asleep before it comes on. When the news is over, I wake up. It happens every day. Even today, decades later, I fall asleep when the news in Sámi is about to come on the radio.

9.

In 1981, the authorities resumed construction along the Áltá-Guovdageaidnu River. The protesters regrouped at Ground Zero. Although the authorities tried to keep their plans secret, we got word that six hundred police were brought to Áltá. They were supposed to live aboard a ship once called *Prinsesse Ragnhild*, which was renamed *Janina* before traveling north. The ship was to be moored at Natokaia.*

A Sámi with a high rank in the Norwegian military (he has died since) secretly asked Mihkkal and me to come to Oslo. Apart from him, we were supposed to meet two foreigners representing an important international organization. This is all we got to know. Mobile phones did not yet exist, and our landlines were tapped. The meeting had to be arranged in complicated ways.

I knew the Sámi from my youth, but we had rarely met as adults. When we came to his house, he greeted us with a big smile. We sat down and had coffee. I wasn't sure what to make of the man. He didn't reveal his political opinions, and his military career was only known to insiders.

Mihkkal made me understand that we had to discuss among ourselves, just the two of us, to assess the situation. I asked our host to excuse us. I said that we needed to be careful, considering what we were discussing. The military

---

* Literally "NATO wharf." Norway was a NATO founding member.

man smiled and said that there were no secret microphones in his house and that we could just go to another room. But Mihkkal preferred to go outside.

Mihkkal asked me whether I thought we could trust the man. I had done some investigating before our visit, but it hadn't produced much. I understood that the man was accustomed to keeping secrets. I also heard that he was an adulterer. When I told Mihkkal, he wasn't too concerned. "Are there Sámi men who aren't?"

We decided to give this a try since we wouldn't get many chances like this.

Back in the house, the man showed us detailed drawings of engine-powered underwater bombs. With them, he said, we could reach *Janina*. He added that the bombs were powerful enough to sink the boat. The water would enter the hull so fast that no pumps would be able to get it out fast enough. "If you agree, I can call two men who can construct the bomb and show you how to use it." Mihkkal got very excited. Before I could even open my mouth, he declared, "Yes, *Janina* will be sunk!"

Our host left to fetch the two men. He returned with them half an hour later. They examined the drawings and discussed them in English. My English wasn't very good at the time, and I couldn't follow everything they said. But I understood that construction required a large magnetic ring, which would help attach the bomb to the ship. Our host told Mihkkal and me that there lay only one challenge in all of this: to operate the underwater bomb at the right depth. The two foreign men explained about how some kind of floating device would help. They said that they could get everything ready within a week, at no cost to us. "Some people with much more money than you will pay," they said with a smile.

We tried to find out how long *Janina* would be moored at Natokaia. Obviously, we needed to get the bomb before the ship was leaving.

When we got back to Álta, *Janina* was already there. We could see that the police were watching for boats to approach it, but no one seemed to expect an underwater attack. But it was all in vain. The delivery of the bomb got delayed, and we never got to sink *Janina*.

Later, the police claimed that they knew about our plans, but I don't believe them. I believe that they just wanted to make it sound like they were doing a good job. Especially for the secret police it was important to look good, because they had so many agents on the ground. Some of them had infiltrated Folkeaksjonen, which is why we didn't trust the Norwegians there (or anybody in the group really). At the time, we kept quiet about this. What we did know was that there were no secret police agents among us Sámi, and we never shared any more information with others than necessary.

I made a couple of trips to *Janina* to see how many police were guarding the ship. Most were at Ground Zero in Stilla. I never saw more than one cop guarding the gangway and two others sitting in a car parked close to it. I had good night-vision binoculars and was able to check the deck closely. They had no cops on watch there. Had we got the bomb in time, it would have been easy to sink the ship.

10.

It is July, and I'm having lunch at Åsgård hospital with Rafter. He is in a particularly good mood. After lunch, we go to his office, where he shows me a letter from the authorities. "You get to go home," he says, smiling.

I read the letter. It's true. After some back and forth, Rafter had been able to convince the authorities to release me from prison after almost five months and let me wait for my trial at home. His argument was that I don't eat in prison due to my fear of being poisoned, and that this caused my health to deteriorate. "I told them that they can't just move you somewhere else to resolve the problem. The only solution is to allow you to be at home. They agreed to that."

I return to prison to get my things. I don't tell anyone that I'm leaving. I just sit there and wait. After a couple of hours, a guard opens the cell door. I assume it's time to go home now, but not quite. I have to see two cops in the interrogation room. One of them is Trygve Eriksen from Fanasgieddi, chief of the secret police in northern Norway; the other is Sverre Opdal from Skoganvarri, the reindeer cop who killed that speckled, unmarked calf I had caught with my lasso. Both speak Sámi. They put pen and paper on the table. "You can go home under one condition: you tell us who the third man in your company was on that night you wanted to blow up the bridge." Trygve Eriksen looks very serious.

"Oh, that suits me just fine," I say. "I can tell you who the third man was." The cops are smiling. I sit down, and Trygve

Eriksen asks again, this time very formally: "Niillas Somby, who was the third man with you that night?"

"Leif Halonen." I keep a straight face, knowing full well that they won't believe me. Leif Halonen is a prominent member of the Labor Party and a strong proponent of the development plans. Trygve Eriksen is, in fact, laughing. "Well. Wasn't it rather Veikko Holmberg?" he tries.

Now, I'm laughing. Then, I say, "Well, nothing will come of this. I gave you a wrong name, and you gave me a wrong name. I don't know who the third man was, so that's it. Have a good day." I get up and head back to my cell. A guard locks the door behind me. I'm enjoying myself, wondering what will come next. It doesn't take long before the guard returns and tells me to get ready. "They'll let you leave anyway." I gather my few things and am ready within minutes.

Trygve is waiting in the office. We take care of some paperwork, and then we head in a taxi to the SAS hotel, where he has booked rooms for us.* He tells me that he will travel all the way to Sirbmá with me and stay there to watch me. Since there are no more flights to Leavdnja today, we'll have to spend a night at the hotel. "Here you'll sleep well, and you have a telephone in your room, so you can make as many calls as you want. You don't have to pay!"

The next morning, when he settles the bill, Trygve seems disappointed that I haven't made any phone calls. "Oh, I forgot," I say, "I'm no longer used to phones."

At Romsa airport, a small crowd is waiting for me. Trygve writes down all their names. At the airport in Leavdnja, a car is waiting for us. Trygve drives me all the

---

* The Scandinavian Airlines System (SAS) is the joint national airline of Denmark, Norway, and Sweden.

way to Sirbmá. Then he continues to the police station in Lákšjohka, where he will reside.

During the coming weeks, I'm under heavy surveillance. Wherever I go, Trygve follows. As soon as I'm in Deanušaldi, I see his car. He seems to be everywhere. I pretend not to realize that I'm being watched. I just smile and say hello when I see him.

11.

I know that the phone at our house is tapped. We have a lávvu close by where the family gathers to chat and drink coffee. It is here that we decide that it was better for me not to stick around for the trial. The authorities still wanted to try John Reier and me under section 148, and we cannot expect a lenient sentence.

My sister has met a man from the Northwest Territories of Canada. She says that the First Nations there have strong self-governance. We discuss this with my brother, who is spending the summer in Sirbmá, and with our friend Bjarne, who visits us frequently. We decide that I will travel to Canada. We have a passport that someone forgot at my sister's house. We also have people on the Finnish side, from which we can make phone calls to Canada without the secret police eavesdropping on us.

Soon, we have a solid plan. I have tickets to Yellowknife and contact details for people who have promised to help me. I haven't spoken English since I worked as a sailor many years ago, but I know enough to manage.

A couple of days before I'm scheduled to leave, I visit the late Knuvta Ovllá in Stuorravuonna to ask for advice. Knuvta Ovllá lights up when I arrive, greets me, and says, "Why do I see a yellow knife, am I going crazy?" I tell them that I have tickets to the town of Yellowknife, and that I have come to ask for help and guidance on my journey.

"You will depart in peace, my friend. They won't see

you, even if they come looking for you. No one will discover that you have left. Your journey will go well, and it is the right decision to leave. You will probably return home one day." Knuvta Ovllá clears his throat and laughs once again about the yellow knife. "Yes, yes, you must really travel to the yellow knife!"

I visit my grandmother and grandfather in Horbmá. I can't tell them that I'm going far away. I'm thinking that this might be the last time I see them. They are both very old, almost a hundred years. Grandfather is sitting in his rocking chair, calmly rolling back and forth. He's come to enjoy this in recent years and no longer hums Laestadian hymns. Instead, he has picked up yoiking—yoiks that I have never heard before. My grandfather, who has always been such a good Christian! He never allowed anyone to yoik. He was very strict. "Yoiking is a great sin!" he used to say. Grandma is as she has always been, kind and hardworking.

I'm getting new, stylish clothes, platform shoes, and thick brown glasses, resembling those of the man whose passport I carry in my pocket. With the platform shoes, I am as tall as him. The pants I bought are long enough to cover the shoes, so that I don't arouse suspicion. The only adjustment I still need to make is to change my hair color to a lighter brown.

There are three of us in the car: Dagny, my sister Marry, and I. Marry is lying down on the back seat, only Dagny and I are visible. Once we have left Sirbmá, I drive as fast as the Volvo will carry us. The speedometer shows 120 miles per hour. Marry and Dagny get scared and plead with me to slow down. I slow down a bit, at least until they get used to the speed.

In Levajok, Bjarne is waiting for us in a red car. I throw my suitcases into it, embrace Dagny and Marry, and then we separate. Bjarne and I are heading for Kárášjohka, Dagny and Marry are returning to Sirbmá. Outside Borsejohka, they met Trygve Eriksen in his car. He sees that there are still two people in our car, is satisfied, and returns to Lákšjohka.

In Kárášjohka, Bjarne and I go to a hairdresser who is waiting for us. She shaves off my beard, colors my hair, and gives me the same haircut as the man in the passport photo. Thereafter, we drive to a cabin by the Anárjohka River near Gáregasnjárga, on the Finnish side. There, another young woman is waiting for us. We spend the night there before we all continue to Roavvenjárga, from where we take a train to Helsinki. The young woman in our company is Bjarne's girlfriend.

In Helsinki we have a couple of hours before it's time to go to the airport. I'm booked on a Finnair flight to Montreal. At the airport, I say goodbye to Bjarne and his girlfriend and head for immigration.

After standing in line for a while, it's my turn. The officer looks carefully at the passport I hand him. Then he looks at me. "Is this really you?"

"Of course," I say. "It's my passport!" I smile as convincingly as I can. The man returns the passport and wishes me a safe journey. Only after I have left his desk do I feel sweat trickling down my forehead.

In Montreal, immigration is a breeze. All the customs officers ask is whether I have brought any meat with me. I'm now in Canada! I sit down and try to light a smoke, but my hands are shaking too much. I must calm down first.

The next day, I continue my journey to Yellowknife. A man by the name of James Wahshee is waiting for me at the airport. I stay in town for a couple of weeks. It is fall and the weather is beautiful. The leaves are turning yellow, just like in Sápmi.

James Wahshee and me in Yellowknife.

One evening, I go to a pub where I meet a descendant of Sámi immigrants. His ancestors came to Canada from Guovdageaidnu and was supposed to teach the Inuit how to herd reindeer. His name is Richard Binder and he works as a plumber.

When I leave Yellowknife, I fly further south, to the town of Letbridge, where Marie Maruli welcomes me. There I also meet the late George Manuel, the most respected Indigenous politician of his generation and a cofounder of the World Council of Indigenous Peoples.[*]

Marie and George make sure that I am well looked after wherever I go in Canada. They spend hours on the phone and finally book me on a flight to Vancouver. They get me new clothes as well. "American ones" since I "can't look like a European," as they laughingly say.

The flight to Vancouver is with Time Air in a small propeller plane. At the airport, George Manuel's son, Arthur,

---

[*] The World Council of Indigenous Peoples (WCIP), founded in Port Alberni on Vancouver Island in 1975, was a global network of Indigenous activists. It dissolved in the mid-1990s.

Bli med på Nils Sombys forunderlige reise

"Join Niillas Somby on his wondrous journey."

is waiting for me with another man. We eat at a Chinese restaurant, and then drive to the home of Arthur's friend, who lives in a large apartment block. As I'm showing them reindeer herding pictures, we hear police sirens approaching. It sounds as if several patrol cars are on their way. Arthur looks out the window and sees that six of them have stopped right in front of the apartment block. He gets nervous and wonders whether the cops are looking for me. Some of them enter the building, and I get scared. But then an ambulance arrives, and paramedics enter. Eventually, they bring out a fellow, and I feel a million times lighter. They had not been coming for me.

I stay in Vancouver for a week. Arthur takes me to a house where other political refugees are staying. They are white South Africans who had to flee their country as supporters of the Black liberation struggle. In the eyes of the regime, they were criminals.

We talk a lot about South Africa while I'm there. They

show me pictures, and I notice that whenever I see Blacks, I also see beer cans. "How can it be that bad when people always have a party?" I ask. It's a typical Kárášjohka joke, and I think I'm being funny, but the South Africans don't laugh. They say that I don't seem to know much about the tactics of the apartheid regime. "The beer cans belong to their most effective weapons. They keep the population drunk and passive. It works very well." They tell me that the cans I see are very cheap and that only Blacks are allowed to buy them. This ensures that they are drunk all the time.

It leaves a big impression on me, and I think about Sápmi. I think of my youth, of how much alcohol I drank, and of how little I knew about the world and politics because of it. I think of the men in Sámi villages who do nothing but drink. Some could have turned out to be great activists had they not become addicted to alcohol. Do the governments of the Nordic countries secretly want the Sámi to get addicted to booze? They certainly don't make much of an effort to keep them away from it. If you're an alcoholic, it's very easy to keep on drinking with the help of government subsidies, whether it's your pension or your welfare check. You can drink all day long, if you want. There and then, I decide that I will never get wasted again. I have only broken that promise once.

12.

George Manuel has found a host for me on Vancouver Island. His ex-wife is coming to pick me up at the home of the South African refugees. We travel by car and ferry to a place called Brentwood Bay, where we meet a man by the name of Philip Paul.

Philip has a wife, Fran, and four boys. Near their home, they have a traditional longhouse, at the edge of the forest. The first few nights I stay at their home, but then they let me move to the longhouse. It's a bit like a lávvu or goahti but constructed of wooden planks. It has a loft, a fireplace, and an adobe floor. I stay there for half a year and hardly leave the premises.

Philip is a serious man, but he has humor, too. Every night he comes around to talk to me about Indigenous spirituality. I would hardly know anything about Indigenous spirituality had I not spent a summer with my grandfather Ásllat at the Buolbmát retirement home. In my youth, this was the only place the municipality offered for the sick and elderly, and it was run by the Sámi Mission.[*]

At first, they wouldn't let me live in the same room as my grandfather, but I insisted that I wanted to stay with him. Eventually, they gave in. Every day, I shaved my grandfather, and he told me about his life.

---

[*] The Sámi Mission of Norway (Norges Samemisjon), founded in 1888, is an Evangelical organization with the aim of Christianizing the Sámi population.

One warm day in the middle of the summer, they found a dead body in the Buolbmát River. The person who had died was my mother's cousin, Kárejon Niillas. Some drunkards had killed him before throwing his body into the river. A few weeks had passed since then, and the body was rotten and smelled terrible.

The morgue was right underneath the room my grandfather and I were staying in. They put the body on a table outside to get the clothes off. The smell spread through the entire nursing home. I felt sick and told my grandfather that we had to move. I considered it impossible to stay there.

"It's just the smell of a dead body, Niillas. We can get rid of it," he said and made some motions with his hand, as if to drive away the smell. Not even a minute later, it was gone. The staff also noticed. "It doesn't smell anymore," I heard someone shout in the hallway. I was amazed and asked my grandfather what he had done. It was the beginning of many lessons in Sámi spirituality, which, after that day, we talked about regularly.

As a teenager, I forgot my grandfather's stories and saw myself as an atheist. I didn't believe in any kind of spirituality. But with Philip Paul so eager to discuss the topic, my grandfather's stories return. Philip and I realize that there are many similarities between the stories of his people and mine. Sometimes we yoik. Philip has a drum and sings traditional Native American songs. He dances, too, and we always have a fire going.

During the day, I go for walks. In the evening, I listen to the radio and read the English dictionary. I have made two good friends in five-year-old Bobby Eliot and eight-year-old Kevin Paul. It's nice to talk to them, and it gives my English a boost.

After a couple of months on Vancouver Island, Bjarne

Philip Paul.

comes to visit me. We light a fire, drink red wine, and dance all evening. Bjarne says that the police in Norway still doesn't know that I have left the country. My sister Marry and my brother Ánde are very skillful in tricking Trygve Eriksen and the entire police force. Ánde calls Marry regularly from Oslo and asks to speak to me. Marry then says that I have just gone for a walk. Sometimes, she is calling out for me but has to conclude that, unfortunately, I am outside right now. Trygve and the police seem satisfied by that, but Bjarne is a media man, and he wants to make a story out of my escape. He intends to let the authorities know that I won't be available for the trial against me. I allow Bjarne to proceed with his plans, and he breaks the news to the *Dagbladet* correspondent in New York City, Arvid Bryne.* This is how everyone in Norway learns that Niillas Somby has escaped.

---

* *Dagbladet*, founded in 1869, is one of Norway's biggest daily newspapers.

13.

Mihkkal Eira and Trygve Eriksen are sitting at the Tostrupkjelleren restaurant in Oslo. There is a bottle of wine on the table, and some fine spirits for Mihkkal. Trygve is in the secret police, but that's not so secret anymore. For many weeks, he has been trying to get Mihkkal, the well-known activist, hunger striker, and friend of mine to talk to him.

Finally, Mihkkal agreed to come to the Grønland police office, an office established for the sole purpose of finding the one-armed man who has escaped. Mihkkal tells Trygve that he might have a thing or two to say about me, but that these matters cannot be discussed in a gray office. This is how they ended up at Tostrupkjelleren in order to chat over a good meal.

Trygve is getting impatient. He has twice tried to bring the conversation to the one-armed man, but Mihkkal never allows others to be in control. "Relax! Let us eat and drink a good glass of wine first, then we can talk about serious things." Trygve understands that there is no use in trying to rush things.

The two have just emptied the third bottle of wine when Mihkkal orders two more. Of course Trygve has to cover the bill. Mihkkal promises him to start talking about the one-armed man soon, but first, he says, he needs to go to the bathroom.

During our hunger strike, Mihkkal became well acquainted with the Tostrupkjelleren staff. Now, he walks up to the doorman and tells him that there is a difficult man at his table. He says that the man has threatened him and challenged him to a fight. The doorman promises to take care of it while Mihkkal is in the bathroom. "Be aware that he pretends to be a policeman!" says Mihkkal. "And make sure he pays the bill before he leaves."

When Mihkkal returns, Trygve has been kicked out.

A few days later, the two meet on the street. Trygve asks Mihkkal once again to talk to him but Mihkkal declines. He says he no longer has any trust in Trygve, since Trygve bailed last time they were trying to talk.

14.

On Vancouver Island, Philip has his own sweat lodge. A sweat lodge is kind of like a steam bath used in spiritual ceremonies.

One day, a man from the northern shores of Vancouver Island arrives. He is a highly respected spiritual healer. Philip invites me to join a sweat lodge ceremony with him.

Philip's sons have been burning fires all day outside the sweat lodge to heat the stones that will be used. Eventually, three of us enter the sweat lodge: the highly respected visitor, Philip, and I. We are only wearing shorts and a towel, but the visitor also carries a drum, two eagle feathers, and a plastic bag with plants. Philip's sons cover the entrance from the outside, and it gets completely dark.

The visitor sprinkles some of the plants onto the hot stones. The embers are almost covered, but he sees to it that there won't be too much smoke. We can smell the plants. Then he starts beating the drum. He is singing, with Philip joining in. I try, too, but the drum and the two men's voices drown out mine.

Philip sprinkles some water on the stones, and the room turns into a sauna. The drumming and the singing continue. The sweat lodge is a tight space, only about three meters wide.

Then, the healer makes sounds that resemble birds flying. I assume he's using the eagle feathers he has brought. The sound gets more and more intense, and I hear him ask an eagle for assistance. He also evokes spirits to come help a young man who has arrived from afar and who had to leave his people. He now sings about an eagle that is with us in the sweat lodge, from which it will take all of the young man's problems to outer space, not allowing them to return. I hear what sounds like an eagle flying around the room, still assuming that the healer is creating the sounds with the feathers he has brought.

Eventually, he makes Paul's sons understand that it is time to open the sweat lodge again. When the boys remove the cover, I see an eagle with us in the sweat lodge. I am astonished.

The healer, who continues to sing, asks Philip and me to leave the sweat lodge. He then follows us, leaving the eagle inside. Still singing, he tells the eagle that it is time to head for outer space, and the eagle obeys and flies away, circling above us, higher and higher, until it is out of sight.

It all seems like a dream to me, and I have to pinch my foot to make sure that I am not asleep. My foot hurts when I pinch it, so I conclude that I am not. When we have lost sight of the eagle, the healer hits the drum one more time very hard and then stops. The singing stops as well.

We stand in silence. Then, Philip takes my hand and says, "Now your problems have gone away."

The healer is sweaty from the singing and drumming. He laughs and says that I am now free to go to town, as nothing can happen to me. "Your problems are gone. You will no longer have to hide." He sounds as if he's joking, but I know he isn't.

I'm taking a trip to Victoria, the main town on Vancouver Island, the very same day. It's strange to no longer hide in the forest and be among people again. It's been a long time. I have a couple of beers and realize that I can no longer have many before getting drunk. I decide to return to Brentwood Bay.

Now I no longer have to hide. I join Philip visiting friends and get to know more people. Philip and I continue with our evening conversations about spirituality. We discuss the sweat lodge ceremony a lot.

One day, five men come to visit Philip. I'm out for a walk, and the boys come running to me and ask me to return to the longhouse. They say that Philip will come there with his guests.

When they arrive, I greet them, and Philip says that they are First Nation elders who have traveled to meet me. We stand in a circle around the fireplace. Philip leads the conversation and talks about me and our conversations about spirituality. Then I tell a little about myself, about where I come from, about Sápmi, about the protests against the Áltá-Guovdageaidnu River dam, and about the failed action at the Fállejohka Bridge. Philip asks me to yoik, and when I finish, the men start singing and beating drums. Finally, one of the visitors speaks. He says that I had to undergo a test, and that I have passed it. They have decided that their First Nation will adopt me in a traditional ceremony. It means that I will belong to this nation, with both the benefits and the responsibilities that come with it. I thank the men for their trust and promise to honor it.

Only later do I understand that the test they were talking about were the evening conversations I've had with Philip.

15.

A week later, two young men, Alvin Nelsson and Hubert, come to pick me up. I'm sad to leave the friends I have made and the house I have stayed in for half a year. But I'm also ready for a change.

We leave in a car, pass through Vancouver, and reach Mount Currie. It is on the Indigenous reserve where the Lil'wat Nation lives. The reserve is located by a river that runs between high mountains. It is roughly the same size as the Deatnu River's largest tributary, the Anárjohka.[*]

Alvin Nelsson has a small boy, and his wife is pregnant with their second child. They have two more boys living with them. Alvin is a talkative man and speaks much faster than Philip. In the beginning, I have problems understanding him, but after a while I get used to it. He lives in a big old timber house, and I get to sleep in the loft.

There are plenty of stray dogs in the village, and you hear them all night. The sounds are familiar. When I close my eyes, I pretend to be in Kárášjohka or some other Sámi town with reindeer-herding dogs.

Alvin is also very interested in Indigenous spirituality, and we discuss it a lot with his kids. We look for deer in the area to hunt, but we only find tracks. They must be close.

---

[*] The banks of the Deatnu River, which constitutes the border between Norway and Finland along a 252 km stretch, are home to significant Sámi communities, many of them salmon fishers.

The mountains are high and the forests dense, it's an unfamiliar landscape for me. I'm also no longer used to long walks, so my feet hurt every time we get back. We visit neighbors frequently, and I befriend many of them. In the evenings, I miss Dagny and the girls, and often shed a few tears.

16.

Alvin's wife gives birth to a little girl, but she only gets to live for a short time because of a heart condition. This causes great sorrow for all of us. When the doctors say that the heart condition is the result of state-run lumber companies having used DDT in the area, it adds yet another dimension to the tragedy. Alvin, who has always lived as tradition- ally as possible, hunts deer to feed his family, and he now believes that this was how his wife ingested the poisonous DDT that affected the newborn's heart. The effects of DDT are long-lasting. When the Canadian government wanted to prove that DDT was safe, they had public officials drink the water in the area. Later, they all died of cancer, and their children were born with missing limbs, without hands, feet, or eyes, or with only one finger. We drive to Vancouver to buy a coffin for the little girl.

A few days later, we have the coffin in the car as we drive to the cemetery to bury her. At the cemetery, we spot a priest. As soon as the car stops, Alvin jumps out and walks up to him. I see the two men talking, before Alvin leads the priest to his vehicle. The priest gets in and drives away. Alvin is agitated. He says that he never asked the priest to come; he only asked the gravedigger to dig a hole. He does not want to have the priest around while grieving. "It is enough that the state has poisoned our animals and killed our children."

Alvin carries the tiny coffin to the grave. We have drums with us and sing. It's a moving ceremony. Alvin talks to the

Brave young men ready to defend their land.

girl and to us. Then we lower the coffin into the grave with
two ropes, cover it with earth, and go home with eyes full
of tears.

The day of my adoption is approaching, and we are driving
toward Williams Lake. Alvin fears that the Royal Canadian
Mounted Police have heard about what is going to happen
and will try to stop us. "But they won't be able to," he says.
Five young men with machine guns sit in the back of our
pickup truck. Should they hear Alvin whistle, they will start
shooting.

Many people have gathered in Williams Lake, mostly from the Indigenous community, but also some white folks. Sulo Lemet Aikio is also there with a Finnish TV crew. A big ceremony is planned.

The elders put white feathers, picked from an eagle's nest, on my head and give me the name Punqwid, which means Mountain Goat Warrior. There are traditional Indigenous dances, and the singing and drumming fill the entire area. There is also lots of great food: salmon in all forms, meat, fruit and vegetables, and an endless supply of cakes. Outside, numerous young men with machine guns stand watch. They have orders to shoot if the police arrive. But the police don't arrive, and we can celebrate in peace.

The First Nation elders say that when Dagny and the girls will arrive next month, they'll be welcomed with a similar ceremony. Sulo Lemet films and interviews me. I tell him that this has been the most extraordinary event in my life.

Several First Nation elders give speeches. Eventually, it's my turn to speak. I'm being filmed by Finnish TV, and I have to speak English, which I still haven't mastered very well, so I'm sweating. But it all goes well.

On the way back to Mount Currie, we are again accompanied by our security guards on the back of the pickup truck. Later, we hear that the police showed up in Williams Lake after we had left, harassing the white folks who were cleaning up. "What were the Indians doing here, and where did they go?"

"We don't know, we only know that they have left," the volunteers answered, while we were driving peacefully toward Mount Currie.

Alvin was still a young man when I met him—he had just turned twenty-five. But he is already an important man in his community, regarding politics and spirituality. Many come to him for consultation, both young and old. He, too, has a sweat lodge, where many spiritual ceremonies are held.

17.

Finally, Dagny and the children arrive. We meet them in Williams Lake. Our Indigenous friends think it's safer that way. They expect the police to follow them.

As promised, there is a welcome ceremony for them, with just as many people turning out as for mine. We have armed guards again, but there is no interference this time. Dagny and the girls get Indigenous names.

Then it's time to say goodbye to Alvin and his people. It's hard to leave new friends yet again.

One of the First Nation elders becomes our new host. For one night, we stay at his house near Williams Lake. The next day, he takes us to a place called Fish Lake. It is largely abandoned. Once, there was an educational center for Indigenous people there. Around the center are six timber houses, which have been empty since the center closed. Some have broken windows and appear run-down, even though they are not that old. But they are full of books, magazines, and newspapers, a reminder of the time when the educational center was still running.

We move into a house that is in pretty good shape. A Polish man, who is married to a Native woman, comes around to fix the water pipes. Then, we are set. We have a fridge and a gas oven. The Polish man and his Indigenous wife are the only neighbors we have. They are quite old, and the Polish man is constantly drunk. But he did a really good job on the water pipes.

Alvin Nelson.

"Don't worry, be happy," is his mantra. He tells us about how he was transporting wood by horse when he first arrived in Canada.

After about a week in our new home, we feel that we've really settled in. But then the chief of the Dakelh Nation, Roger Jimmie, pays us a visit and tells us to get ready to leave as quickly as possible. Police have been spotted in the reserve, and people are worried that they are looking for us. *Dagbladet* in Norway has reported that Dagny and the girls are now staying with me.

We don't even have time to say goodbye to our neighbors. We drive all night. In the morning, we arrive in the hamlet of Biziko, where Roger Jimmie has a house and a family. Biziko is very isolated, at the end of a forest road. Apart from Roger's house, there is only one more. "You'll be going even more remote," he says.

We spend a night at his place and have thick American pancakes with syrup and other treats for breakfast. While we adults talk, the children go outside to play. Our girls don't speak English, but Roger's boys get Risten to drive

Anja and Risten in Fish Lake.

a children's snowmobile on a frozen pond. We watch her as she drives round and round. The boys are on a bigger snowmobile and have Anja with them. Eventually, Risten gets off the snowmobile and walks toward the house, but the boys follow her, pull her up on their snowmobile, and return her to the smaller one. They fill it up with petrol, and Risten continues driving.

Eventually, she drives by the house several times, yelling something that we can't hear. I go outside, and Risten yells that she no longer wants to drive. I tell her that the snowmobile will stop automatically if she lets go of the handlebars. Risten follows my advice and finally makes her escape from endless snowmobile riding. But not for long, since Roger is taking us by snowmobile to a hamlet called Kluskus, far off the beaten track. There are no roads leading there, and we ride our snowmobiles all day.

18.

Kluskus consists of nothing but a small wooden cabin, a paddock with two horses, an outhouse, and a woodshed. The surroundings remind me of northern Finland, with pine trees, swamps, and lakes. Near the cabin is a pond. It has no fish but plenty of beavers.

We will be staying with the man who owns the cabin, Loyd Boyd. He is a sixty-year-old Indigenous man, slim and strong. Loyd is divorced and lives with his fifteen-year-old daughter, Loraine. He also has two sons, Arnold and Dany, but they live elsewhere. Loyd is Roger Jimmy's father-in-law. His house has two bedrooms and a large open space, which serves both as a living room and a kitchen. Loraine also sleeps there. Loyd tells us that the main settlement of the reserve is two miles away, and it has six houses and a school.

So, Loyd and Loraine are our new hosts. In the evenings, we like to be outside and listen to the sound of nature. We hear wolves howling, and I think that this is what it must have been like in Sápmi when there were still wolves around.[*]

The people from the reserve hear about us. They come around to visit, arriving in turns, all on snowmobiles. We get to know everyone and are invited to visit the main

---

[*] Increased human settlement and hunting brought the wolf population of the Nordic countries close to extinction in the late nineteenth century. Today, there is a population of about eight hundred wolves in the central and southern parts of the Nordic countries but not in Sápmi.

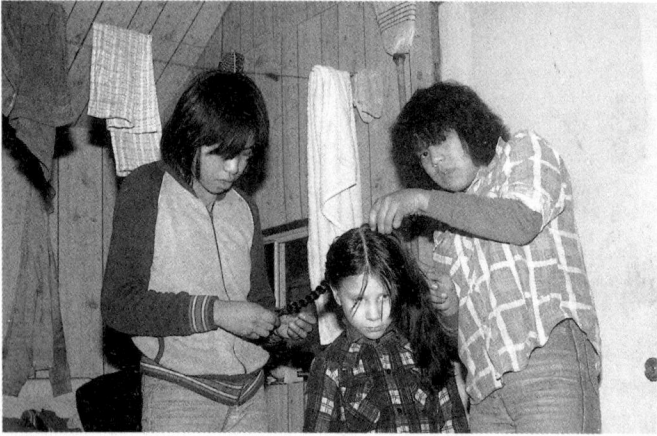

Loraine and Sandra get Anja ready for school.

settlement and the school that our girls will attend. We travel there on Loyd's snowmobiles, visit all the houses and meet the teachers, two young white folks, who warmly welcome Anja and Risten.

When school starts, Anja and Risten walk there with Loraine, who is still in school as well. It only takes a few weeks for the girls to speak English as well as their peers. They get coupons with Smurfs as a reward for not using snuff, which almost all of the other kids in school do. With the coupons, they can buy things at the school's little store.

When spring comes, Loyd hands Loraine a 32-caliber revolver. He tells her to carry it to and from school because grizzly bears might attack. Loyd gives Loraine shooting lessons and they test the weapon. He is adamant that she always needs to have the revolver ready.

Weapons are nothing new to Loraine, but Risten and Anja get scared when they see how powerful the revolver is. Loyd stresses how dangerous it is to come across a bear with cubs, especially when it has just come out of hibernation.

Loyd blows up a beaver dam to prevent his cabin from being flooded.

One evening, Dagny and I go for a walk in the forest. It is just getting dark when we hear a bear roaring behind us. It sounds a little like a cow mooing, but we know that there are no cows here, so it must be a bear. Dagny, who usually walks slowly and absorbs everything she comes across, begins to hurry. So do I, especially because we hear yet another bear, now on the other side of the path. We have guns with us but decide that it's best to flee. The bears follow us and seem to communicate with one another. Only when we're very close to the cabin do they back off.

When the bears come out of hibernation, we have to be aware of what we have around the cabin. Loyd reminds us that if we hang a deer hide outside, the bears will smell it and come looking for food. He also makes sure that no traces of the moose he shot during the winter remain anywhere near the cabin.

In the outhouse, Loyd stores plenty of dynamite, which he uses to blow up the beaver dams. This is to avoid flooding; a swamp can quickly turn into a lake. Not far from Loyd's

My sister is visiting.

cabin, a cabin flooded because no one destroyed the beaver dams in its vicinity.

Loyd hunts lynx with traps, and I often join him to check on them. When I am with him, they are always empty. But one day, when I go by myself, I find a trapped lynx that is trying to pounce at me. It bares its teeth and snarls. When I shoot it in the head, it falls to the ground. I'm pulling it back to the cabin like I would do with a reindeer calf. But Loyd is not too happy about me dragging the lynx through the snow, as the fur takes damage. He is generous about it. He just says that, next time, I must not shoot the lynx but strangle it, and I must not drag but carry it. The fur must remain in the best condition possible.

One day, Roger arrives with my sister Marry. Loyd is out hunting moose. Marry has traveled all the way from Sápmi to visit us. She has brought sweets for the kids and other presents. Risten, who loves candy, eats a whole package. Then she feels ill, probably because she's no longer used to candy.

When Loyd returns with a moose, we use parts of the

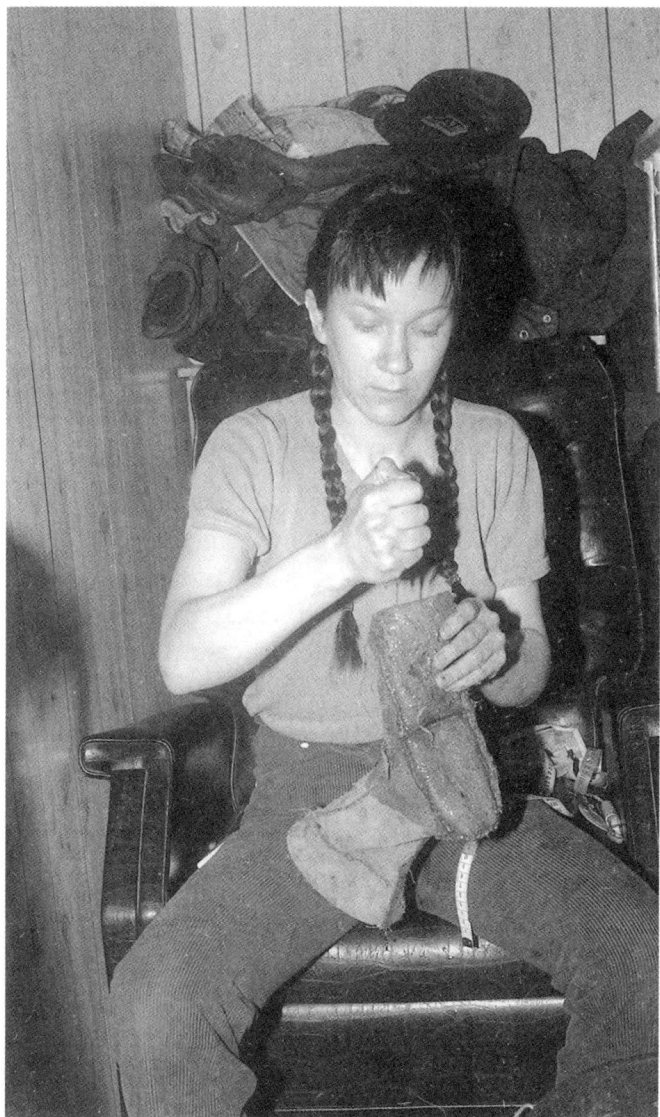

Dagny makes *gámmagat* from moose skin.

Little girls slaughtering big animals.

meat to make soup, and Marry uses some of the blood to make sausage. We eat bone marrow and use more of the blood to make patties. My sister is not visiting every day, so we figure we'll have a feast. Loyd is amazed that we are able to make all these dishes. It's Indigenous knowledge that he feels his people have lost.

I'm excited to hear news from home. Kluskus is not very modern. We have no telephone and have heard nothing from Sápmi since Dagny arrived. We have a good laugh when Marry tells us how she and Ánde turned the police's wiretapping against themselves.

Dagny makes *gámmagat*, traditional Sámi shoes, out of the moose fur that Loyd has brought back home. Roger and Loyd also get gámmagat. The people of the village inspect them carefully. Dagny also makes a pretty handbag and a belt from tanned moose skin, which is quite thick. We smoke some of the moose meat and it tastes delicious. Loyd says that he has never done that himself.

One day, we go on a fishing trip with him. He cuts a large hole in the ice of a frozen lake with a chainsaw. The chainsaw

Handling an ax with one hand.

seems to be his favorite weapon. He also cuts moose meat with it. Luckily, he doesn't use gasoline for everything.

We get fish in abundance, and on the way home we stop by the reserve's main settlement to share our catch. People on the reserve always share what they fish and hunt. They don't ask for anything in return. We often receive fish and meat from others.

In the summer, I also go moose hunting, since Loyd has encouraged me to do so. In the beginning, I find none, only tracks. Whenever I catch a glimpse of one, it disappears in a heartbeat. Two weeks go by, and I have not fired a single shot. Loyd tells me that I'm probably out at the wrong time of day. He tells me to go hunt at dawn or dusk.

The next day, I get up early, before it is light. I prepare the gun inside the house—and it goes off! The bullet leaves a big hole in the door. I suppose my eye was still too tired and my hand too stiff. Miraculously, no one woke up, and I rush out into the forest.

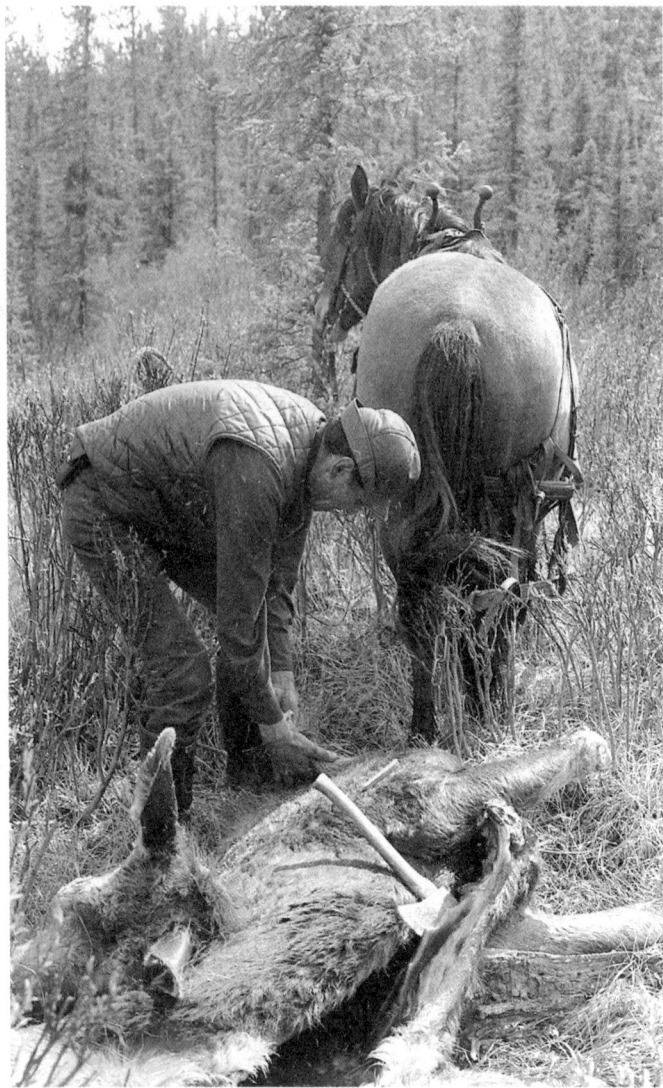

We transport the moose home by horse.

Time for laundry.

Loyd was right. I quickly find a fat two-year-old cow and shoot it. For two weeks, we have only been eating spaghetti since the meat from earlier hunts has run out. So, the joy over me reporting a successful hunt is greater than the anger over the hole in the door. In fact, Loyd just laughs it off. He gets one of the horses to fetch the moose. Over the following weeks, I turn into a good moose hunter and always get us meat when we need it.

Most of the meat from my first hunt we hang up to dry, but we salt it too much. We have to wash off the salt and dry the meat again. It ends up tasting really good. Of course, the other people on the reserve get their share.

On occasion, the people on the reserve travel to Kluskus. Usually, they all go together. At times, our family are the only ones staying. We act like colonialists and give the places around Kluskus familiar names, such as Divganjeaggi.*

One day, we notice a big bird flying over the cabin. In the evening, the girls find an owl stuck in the barbed wire

---

* Divganjeaggi is the name of a swamp not far from the Somby family's home in Sápmi.

The big owl that avoided having its head chopped off.

fence that Loyd has put up to protect the cabin from bears. We try to free the owl, but it is angry and attacks us. I hit it over the head with a stick, then it is calm. We get it loose, take a picture, and put it on a table in front of the house.

When I go to the outhouse, I feel the lifeless bird's eyes watching me. I get a big knife from the cabin to chop off its head. But the moment I lift the knife over its head, it flies away. I'm left puzzled, holding the knife above my head ready to chop while the bird circles over our cabin before it disappears.

Another day, the girls tell me that they've seen owls in a hole in the ground near the cabin. They also say that they've seen strangers who were dressed like Sámi. Dagny and I follow them, but we find nothing. The strangers never return.

School holidays begin in the middle of summer. Everyone from the reserve is going into town that day. While they are gone, it starts to rain. There is thunder and lightning, and soon we're in the middle of the worst thunderstorm I've ever seen.

Hunting girls with prey.

The rain doesn't stop for two weeks, and the entire area gets flooded. No one is returning from town. We assume that the rain has destroyed the road. We are out of flour and most dry goods. All we have left is spaghetti and salt. Anja has found a way to bake bread from spaghetti. She soaks the pasta until it gets doughy and then adds dry yeast and salt. The bread tastes good, and Anja is very proud.

We have set up a lávvu, hidden away in the forest, so we have a place to retreat to if anyone is coming to look for us, or when Loyd has guests we don't want to be seen by. Government officials and teachers usually arrive in a small plane that lands on a lake nearby; it is impossible to miss the plane landing, which gives us time to go to the lávvu.

We get so tired of eating spaghetti that we develop new ways of hunting. For example, we use snares to catch rabbits along the edge of the swamp. We don't kill more than we can eat. We decide not to hunt moose while we wait for the people from the reserve to return. If we kill moose, we want to share it, and we are also almost out of bullets. But when no one has returned after three weeks and the children have

The girls get to know the horse well.

grown tired of eating rabbits, I decide to get us a moose,
nonetheless. I have to be very careful with the few bullets
we have left.

All goes well, and I kill a moose. But now I have to get
it to the cabin! I have never saddled a horse before. Luckily,
Risten and Anja have been attentively watching Loraine, so
they guide me through the process. We bring the moose to
the house. It is so heavy that we are unable to turn it onto
its back. It lies on its side while we gut it. We have to use the
horses to move the carcass, and they are very obedient, so
we manage. We get a lot of meat. Since the people from the
reserve haven't arrived yet, we smoke it all.

I saved the empty cartridge from the hunt. I flatten it
and attach a crook to it that I found in the cabin. Now, we
have a hook we can use for fishing. Anja and I go to the river
on the other side of the settlement. We get there in the dark.
There are some abandoned cabins, and we plan to spend the
night. But I don't get any sleep due to the mosquitoes. I'm
up all night making sure that Anja isn't getting bitten.

In the morning, we go to the riverbank. There are no mosquitoes there. We catch fish every time we throw the hook into the water. Often it is what our hosts call "squaw-fish," and we give it to the dogs. But we get plenty of trout as well.

19.

Now, we have very good food: smoked meat, fresh fish, and bread made from soaked spaghetti dough.

One morning, we hear a plane circling over the cabin. First once, then twice. It is clear that it intends to land on the lake. We leave everything behind and run to the lávvu. We have two black dogs with us: one is quick and clever, the other slow and stupid.

We huddle in the lávvu and wait, hoping the plane might take off again. But it doesn't. Suddenly, one of the dogs is gone. It has gnawed through the rope that we tied it to and runs at full speed toward the house. I am worried that it will lead the people from the plane to us, as I assume that they are somewhere around the cabin. And, indeed, soon we hear steps approaching. We are very scared, but: it is only Roger! We are happy and relieved when we see him. "Have you moved in here?" Roger laughs. "In any case, you have a very good dog. It ran to me when I called it!"

Roger has company. It's Nils Gunnar Lie from Norwegian TV. Nils Gunnar is here with Bjarne's permission. He seems a little concerned because he has been to the outhouse. I tell him the dynamite is only there to blow up beaver dams.

Nils Gunnar brings very good news. The Norwegian authorities are no longer trying John Reier and me under section 148. John Reier has already had his trial in Hámmárfeasta and got a prison sentence of only five months. He was able to go home right away, since he had already served his time on remand at the prison in Čáhcesuolu. Nils Gunnar Lie has come to ask us whether we want to go home under these circumstances. I feel a great burden lifted off my shoulders, but I know that if I had stayed in Sápmi they would have tried us under section 148 and that we would have been handed harsh sentences.

I go for a walk in the forest by myself. I thank the eagle who took all my problems away. I thank Bjarne, who has helped me so much and has shown so much courage. I thank my brother Ánde and my sister Marry. I thank Dagny and my two little girls. I thank Philip, Alvin, George, Loyd, Roger, Knuvta Ovllá, Björn Rafter, and everyone else who has assisted me during these difficult times.

Our friendly black dog is not one to bark and howl. But one night he doesn't stop, and we can't sleep. The next morning, when I check Loyd's lynx traps, I understand why. The dog got caught in one of them. His leg is shattered, and he was trying to gnaw through the trap all night. With a heavy heart, I shoot him.

The other dog has also disappeared—as mysteriously as it had come. Life feels strange and empty without the dogs; we got used to them.

I sit and have a smoke. Without thinking, I throw the burning cigarette butt into the grass. Then I go to the cabin. When I come outside again, I see smoke coming from the riverbank. Did the cigarette butt set the dry grass on fire? I rush to the riverbank and realize that the fire has already spread in various directions. I run back to the house and get a bucket of water. I call for the girls to help. Dagny stays inside finishing another pair of *gámmagat*.

We try to put out the fire by throwing water on it but soon understand that it is pointless. The fire is eating its way

Forest fire in Kluskus.

through the grass, and the highest flames are already reaching the tops of the pine trees. We are scared and desperate. What if the fire department and the police have to be called in? And what about the hay that Loyd has stacked along the swamp? The fire will soon be there, and the smoke is getting thicker by the minute.

The girls cry, run to their mother, and complain about their stupid father. Dagny comes out and takes a sober look at things. She says that we should consider ourselves lucky. The fire is neither heading for our cabin nor for the Kluskus settlement. But the pine trees are in danger, and a serious forest fire is a possibility. Loyd's haystack seems lost. We watch the scene with teary eyes.

At dusk, it starts to rain, and the fire goes out. I go down to the swamp. A big area has turned completely black. Only the poles remain of Loyd's haystack. But under the circumstances I feel relieved, because the forest hasn't burned down and there are no more embers. I assume that Loyd will throw us out of the cabin, considering the damage I have caused. I wait in fear for his return.

Loyd returns a week later. The first thing he does is let the horses loose. "I can see you've had a fire," he says and pours himself some coffee. He proceeds to explain that the area will soon be green and lush, and that his people have often burned parts of it to renew natural growth. "When you burn the land, you get a lot of grass and herbs, which attract animals. You lose some forest, but that only keeps the logging companies away. A few years after the fire, there'll be many new pine trees, which serve as great building material and natural fuel."

"But what about the hay?" I ask.

"Didn't you see that I let the horses loose? They'll find food themselves, and they won't run away. We can always get them if we need them."

We have grown familiar with both the area and the people, and it seems difficult to leave. But we get a call from the Nuxalk people who are asking us to come to Bella Coola. First Nation leaders have made an agreement with the authorities. We no longer have to hide. We can stay in Canada in peace, as long as we don't make any fuss.

Fall has returned and there is already snow on the ground, when Loyd Boyd gets his two horses ready to pull us in a wagon to Biziki. His son Dany lives there with his wife. Roger Jimmie also has a house there. There's a decent trail for the wagon leading to Biziki.

20.

We are fetched by the late Lawrence Pootlass, who is accompanied by Robert Andy. Robert is a muscular man. Lawrence, the head of the Nuxalk people, is short and slender. They call themselves "salmon people" and have come to take us to Bella Coola.

After an eight-hour journey, we descend from the mountains along a windy road. Only this part takes us an hour. After passing through a river valley, we reach the coast and, finally, Bella Coola. I am not pleased to learn that Norwegian immigrants once took control of the entire valley, including the road. I always thought that Norwegians only took control of Sápmi, but clearly they also occupied the best lands of the Nuxalk people.

Amalie Pootlass.

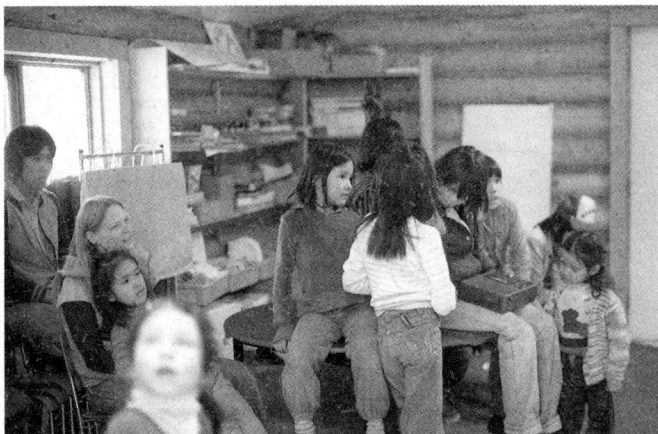

At school in Kluskus.

The Norwegians arrived here three to four generations ago and worked in agriculture and logging. They built large houses and established farms. As Lawrence and Robert tell us, the Canadian government sold the land to them even though it was the traditional land of their people. Today, the Nuxalk people only have control over the lower part of the river.

In the town of Bella Coola, we get to live in our own house. The location is great, and it doesn't take us long to socialize. Everyone invites us for coffee and good meals.

Bella Coola and Kluskus are two different worlds. In Bella Coola, there are cars and all sorts of modern facilities. We had just gotten used to life off the beaten track! The children find new playmates easily. Their English is better than that of their parents.

The Bella Coola River has an abundance of salmon. We eat lots of it: roasted, dried, boiled, and in all sorts of other ways. I get to join crews fishing with nets. In Sápmi, along the Deatnu River, we also fish salmon with nets. But here, the net is much shorter. There is a lot of clay in the water,

Drying salmon.

Frying salmon.

which makes the water look like blue-green milk. The fishers take the boats up the river on pickup trucks. "We don't want to travel upriver with noisy engines and disrupt the wildlife. We all have cars, so why not transport the boats with them?"

Usually, we don't need to wait long before the nets fill up with salmon. I'm surprised that the fishers here don't take the salmon out of the nets immediately, as we do along

Fishing nets are used without permission from the authorities.

the Deatnu. With all the splashing salmon in the nets, the water gets rough. But the nets aren't brought in until they are so full that they threaten to sink. Once they've been pulled up, there are salmon everywhere on the boat. When the boat returns to the wharf, the salmon is loaded on pickup trucks. That marks the end of a fishing day.

I am told that six different types of salmon come to the river every year. First, there is the chinook or spring salmon, large and similar to the Atlantic salmon. Then comes the sockeye salmon. It is smaller, but there are many of them. They are usually canned and kept as food for the winter. The kind that is known in Sápmi as Pacific salmon also comes to the river. It's the same kind that migrates up the Deatnu and other salmon-carrying rivers in Sápmi. Its meat is less red than that of other salmon, and it tastes good when you boil it, serving as a welcome alternative when you have overdosed on the red kind. Finally, there is the kind that everyone knows from TV. Chum salmon, which they call "dog salmon" here. It travels up the river to spawn, and then it dies. Chum salmon usually don't appear before the fall. If they do, the smell is terrible, because after they have spawned and die, they rot. Predators—bears, eagles, and other birds—follow them. One time, I met a wolf at the riverbank. I had a camera with me, but the wolf was faster.

You don't fish for chum salmon in the river but in the sea. Both Natives and whites do it. They need to get permits, similar to the fishing quotas that exist on the Norwegian side of Sápmi. Everything is strictly regulated by the Canadian authorities.

For many people here, sea salmon fishing is the most important source of income, but many Nuxalk sell their quotas. The Nuxalk are not fond of salty fish, and I never saw any of them prepare or eat salmon.

Occasionally, other types of fish also get caught in the nets, especially steelheads. They are related to the Atlantic salmon. Natives are allowed to keep them, but whites must throw them back into the water, whether they are alive or dead.

The Nuxalk people have an agreement with the Canadian government that obligates the authorities to keep the fish population healthy. Logging on the upper bank of the Bella Coola River destroyed the spawning grounds, and the salmon population in the river began to decline. Today, there are fish farming facilities. Eggs and milt are taken from the salmon to produce fingerlings, which are released back into the river. This is how the different salmon populations survive. There is an overabundance of fish in the water today.

I take a tour to see the farms. The workers, most of them young people from the area, mark out the river with fences. Every half hour, they add another fence downstream. In no time, they catch hundreds of salmon.

The work reminds me of marking reindeer calves. First, the workers sort out the fish that do not belong to the stock they are working with and release them back into the river. The fish they keep they kill, and the eggs and milt are placed in clean plastic pouches. Then comes the next load into the fence, the process is repeated, and so on.

I talk to the boss of one of the farms, a man who says to be of northern Finnish and Sámi descent. He tells me about the work in detail. When I ask him about diseases, he says that the fish are monitored. If any dead ones float to the top, samples are taken instantly in the entire area. He says that the system works and that they haven't had a single serious disease outbreak. I watch the workers put milt on the eggs. They need to wet the eggs first, only then can the milt fertilize them.

So many tourists come to see the farms that the farms employ their own tour guides. The tourists like to stop by the rubbish dump because there are always some bears rummaging around, with not much concern for people coming close.

The Nuxalk are very protective of their rights. They do not allow logging companies on their lands. Tourists aren't allowed to fish in their waters either. And children aren't allowed to play in the fishing grounds; it's considered a bad habit, like playing with food.

The Nuxalk are traditional, spiritual people. Every year, before the salmon fishing season starts, they hold a cere- mony led by their chief and involving the elders as well as spiritual healers. During the ceremony, fish that were caught beforehand are released back into the river to honor the river's patron spirit. They are wrapped in bark and released into the river in small boats, also made of bark.

The ceremony begins with the chief dancing alone, while young men sing and beat drums. In his song, the chief thanks the river's patron spirit. When the song ends, two young men wade into the river and release the fish at a spot chosen by the chief. Thereafter, there is more singing, dancing, and drumming. When the ceremony ends, the fishing season can begin.

The season lasts as long as the fish that are caught can be used. This includes distribution among the elderly, the sick, and alcoholics. Then there is no more fishing. Fish are not seen as a commodity. It is not legally prohibited to continue fishing, but everyone knows when it's time to stop. The Nuxalk people do it in the same spirit that keeps them from riding their motorboats upstream.

In important matters on the reserve, the elders are asked for advice. In that case, they gather for a meeting, over which the chief presides. He has an assistant among whose tasks it is to communicate with government authorities. Finances, education, health, and welfare are all handled by the reserve's own administration.

In 2004, Robert Andy from the Nuxalk elders' council came to visit me in Sápmi. He took part in a seminar on salmon fishing that we organized in Sirbmá, Luosnjárga, and Ohcejohka. Before he returned to Canada, he wrote a letter to the Norwegian Sámi Parliament, asking Sámi politicians for help in fighting the Norwegian fish farming industry, which is making inroads into Nuxalk territory. The Norwegian fish farms breed Atlantic salmon, which is stronger than Pacific salmon. Wherever Atlantic salmon spreads, it wipes out the local salmon population. Robert Andy never received a reply from the Sámi Parliament, and no Sámi politician has ever become active in the matter.

Today, we can see that the Norwegian fish farming industry has caused much havoc in Nuxalk territory.

The salmon population in the Bella Coola River has been greatly reduced. In 2012, a member of the Norwegian Sámi Parliament joined a government delegation from Norway at a seminar in Canada to discuss the effects of the Norwegian fish farming industry. I tried to find out what he said at the seminar but never got a straight answer from the Sámi Parliament. I got an answer from him to a message on Facebook but he claimed that he had lost his notes. He emphasized that he would "of course" support the Nuxalk people. This happened at a time when the Labor Party was in power in Norway and also held the majority of the seats in the Sámi Parliament.

21.

In the fall, Bjarne comes to visit us in Bella Coola. He has moved to Canada because he has met Ester, an Indigenous woman of the Blackfoot Nation. They live in Alberta. Ester accompanies Bjarne on his visit. Bjarne tells us that he has been asked by Canadian TV if he can arrange permission for a short documentary film about our family.

We turn to Lawrence, one of the elders, for advice. We explain that we are no longer afraid of being deported to Norway, as the charges against me have been significantly reduced. We also explain that the Canadian government has agreed not to deport us, as long as we don't make a fuss. We've also been promised residency in Canada after a stay of five years.

For the First Nations, their own customary laws are very important. They feel that they should be able to adopt and grant residency to whoever they want, and that this should be accepted by the Canadian government. Lawrence gathers all elders for a meeting. They decide that Canadian TV can film a documentary about us.

Two weeks later, Bjarne returns with a television crew. We scout locations. When we return, we notice police cars driving past our house. Everyone in Bella Coola has seen them, and within an hour hundreds of people have gathered outside our home to protect us. The police come around one more time but realize that they won't be able to execute any orders that day.

The television crew stays for half a week. They interview Dagny and me as well as Lawrence and Bjarne. They focus a lot on the question of whether First Nations should have the right to grant residency permits to foreigners according to their customary laws. It is clear that our presence has now created a fuss and that we have violated the agreement with the government.

We decide to travel with Bjarne to Alberta. Before we leave Bella Coola, we are presented with twelve salmon that young men have fished from the river. Bjarne and I salt and pack them. We are driving all the way to Alberta in Bjarne's pickup truck. The police stop us once for speeding, but we don't get a ticket. When we arrive in Alberta, we want to eat the salmon but it's too salty. We wash it off in the bathtub, not knowing that the tap water contains chlorine. The water turns red, the salmon turns pale, and we have to throw it out.

Dagny and I are prepared to be arrested and sent home. It's okay. We feel that it's time to return to Sápmi. My sister Marry has fallen ill, and my parents are struggling. We tell the girls not to talk to the police when we get arrested.

22.

One afternoon, we notice police slowly driving past Bjarne's house. We wonder whether they're coming for us. Early next morning, there is a violent knock on the door. As soon as I open it, two cops grab me by the neck. They won't even let me put on my shoes before pulling me into their van. I see Dagny being shoved into another van, and our daughters, who are crying, into a car. We are taken into custody. Dagny and I are brought to prison and housed in separate units. We don't know where they take the kids.

The prison is modern and feels more like an airport terminal. You can walk around in a large common room with five TV screens, all showing different programs. There, I get to see the television program about us (produced by a man called Denis Macintosh) together with other prisoners, most of them Indigenous people arrested for driving under the influence.

I'm taken to a court hearing in the prison's basement. It's only me, two cops, and a judge. I am sentenced to one week in prison awaiting trial. Two days later, I'm allowed to call Bjarne. He tells me that they had to release Dagny because the girls wouldn't say a single word to anyone. The authorities didn't know what to do and let Dagny and the girls return to Bjarne's house.

The prisoners in my unit are divided into different groups. I quickly find the one that suits me best. It's a group of Indigenous people with a good sense of humor. One of them is married to a white woman and is asked by the others how it is working out. "Fine," he says. "There is just one problem: my wife gets dirty so quickly that she has to bathe every day, and while that's her business, she insists on me taking a bath every day, too."

There is one old white man in the group. He likes to talk. He tells everyone that he got unlucky when he married the wrong woman. He insists that you should never be deceived by the looks of a woman. According to him, looks are not important. He says that the most important thing is how a woman reacts when she gets angry. In order to find out, he says, you need to test her. His advice is to come home drunk one morning and make enough noise to wake her up. Then you lie down in the hallway and pretend to be asleep. Her reaction, he insists, will tell you what kind of a partner she is. "Avoid pretty women like the plague!" He insists that this is the lesson he has learned and claims that he became homeless only after he was kicked out by his temperamental wife. Now, he is an alcoholic and has been homeless for ten years because this woman had made his life so difficult. "Every fall, I break a couple of shop windows, so that I get arrested and put into prison, where it is warm, I get hot meals every day and have good company. It also helps to sober up once a year!"

After one week, I return to court and am sentenced to another week behind bars. I am not surprised. Since my time in prison in Norway, I am used to receiving the same sentence over and over again. The intention, of course, is to break people down. They want you to count the days until your release, only to put you back to square one.

I call Bjarne, who tells me that the Assembly of First Nations has sent a letter to the court, vouching for me. They assure the court that Niillas Somby won't escape but stand trial. They emphasize that First Nations have the right to grant foreigners residency permits, and they demand my release. A trial doesn't bother them, as it will provide them with the opportunity to make their case in court. I have learned my share about the legal system and I don't think that the Assembly of First Nations letter will make much difference, but I am touched by their efforts.

At my next court hearing, Bjarne is present. He reads the letter to the judge and then hands it to him. The judge looks it over once more and says, "It's a well-written letter, but you cannot trust what the Indians write and say." I expected the court to reject the letter's demands, but I did not expect the judge to be so openly racist. I am furious. When it is my turn to speak, I object to the judge's racist statement and state that it should be documented in the record.

I receive the same sentence as usual, another week in detention. I declare that I cannot do anything to change the sentence but will go on hunger strike in protest. Bjarne, who is a media man, writes a press release. Soon thereafter, journalists from Canadian newspapers, radio, and TV stations start calling me in prison. My hunger strike becomes a big story, partly because hunger strikes are uncommon in Canada, and partly because our family has just been on national television. I use the interest to tell everyone about the racist comment by the judge, the rights of Indigenous people, and the whiteness of Canada's government. I also explain that the lands of the Indigenous peoples have been robbed by folks who had no more claim to those lands than the dirt under their fingernails when they arrived on the continent.

They serve good food in prison. But I'm only having a glass of water, sitting at a table on my own, as usual. Two prison guards come over and ask me why I'm not eating. I point at the water and say that water is also food. "You are on hunger strike. We will have to arrest you because hunger strikes are illegal."

The inmates closest to me start laughing. "Someone is going to be arrested in prison? That's something new!" The prison guards don't laugh. They take me to the warden's office area, from where you can see all units: the men's, the women's, and the youth's. The area has both a big open space and individual rooms. The guards lock me into one of the rooms. I have to hand over everything I carry. I hand over a one-liter can of tobacco (I only stopped smoking later), matches, and a few other things. Then they tell me to take off my clothes. They order me to wear a prison suit that looks like a nightgown. The room I'm in has a bed and huge windows on all sides. When I'm lying in bed, guards can see me from wherever they are. They bring me food, and I put a pillow over it, since I'm hungry and I don't want to smell the food. The guards come and take all pillows away. They leave the food and only exchange the plate when it's time for dinner and they bring a new one.

I want to smoke and press the button I was told to press when I needed to go to the bathroom. A guard comes in and I ask him nicely if I can have a smoke. "You can smoke when you eat something," he says and smirks. "Okay, then I won't smoke," I say. I'm in a very bad mood. I'm sweating, trembling, and freezing all at the same time, because my body yearns for nicotine.

Suddenly, a man in a white coat enters the room. He is carrying medical equipment. He introduces himself as a nurse who is going to monitor my health while I'm on hunger strike. He takes my blood pressure, temperature, and pulse. At first, I appreciate that he is looking after me. But when this man and his colleagues take turns in visiting me every other hour, I realize that the care they offer is actually harassment. At night, I can't get any sleep. They come into the room constantly. Suffering another bout of serious nicotine withdrawal, I have had enough. "You can no longer come in here and bother me!"

"Are you serious?"

"Yes. Get the hell out of here and stop playing with me! You know just as well as I that you are not here to help me. All you do is harass me!"

The nurse, who used to be friendly and chatty, sighs. "I'm sorry it has turned out that way. My whole day has been bad, and now you're acting up, too. From now on, I will have to ask the guards to restrain you when I come in here."

"Sure, bring them along—and the biggest monkeys you can find!"

After the nurse has left, I regret my outburst. Now, there'll be a fight with the guards every two hours, and I have no chance of winning. All just for tobacco, one of their weapons. I'm upset and decide to apologize.

When the nurse returns, he has two gigantic guards with him, who stand in the doorway. I do as planned: I apologize and state that I am a slave to tobacco, which was the reason for my behavior. I make it clear that he and his colleagues can do check-ups whenever they deem them necessary.

The nurse seems happy and sends the two giants away. The giants, on the other hand, don't look happy at all. I think they were looking forward to some action. "Are you sure you'll be fine by yourself?" one of them asks the nurse. When the nurse confirms, they leave. With them, my cravings for nicotine also disappear. I have never had a craving for a cigarette since.

23.

After a week in the windowed room, it is time to go to court again. I'm thinking about kicking the tobacco tin in the air when they hand it back to me but conclude that this is not a good idea. That day, I eat the breakfast. It doesn't take long before a guard lets me out of the room since I have eaten. My hunger strike seems to have made some impact. At least indirectly. I have been able to tell all of Canada that the judge was a racist, and my case has received international attention. Despite it all, I get sentenced to another week in detention.

Finally, it's time for the trial. A lot of Indigenous people have come. Most are from Bella Coola, but there are also representatives from the Assembly of First Nations. The verdict doesn't surprise anyone. The Somby family will be sent back to Norway and banned from Canada for life. We are supposed to leave the country the day after the verdict.

The next morning, I am driven to the airport in a large, black car. Dagny and the girls are already there. They are wearing traditional Sámi dresses.

A policeman accompanies us to Oslo. He is elderly and kind. No one on the plane seems to notice that we are prisoners. We occupy the last rows.

In Oslo, a crowd is waiting for us at the airport. Most are Sámi activists or journalists. We are only allowed to talk to the journalists, but one of them is a close relative of mine, Magne Ove Varsi. He's not afraid of the police and greets us heartily. After we've talked to the journalists, we are taken to the Grønland police station.

The police in Oslo are well-prepared for our arrival. They interrogate us. They have brought in Nils Henriksen, a Sámi-speaking officer from Guovdageaidnu. I am a little surprised that they no longer ask about the third man at the Fállejohka Bridge. They only ask me things they already know. They are not aggressive either, and we can have a normal conversation. I assume that Henriksen has much to do with it. He's a fine fellow. The interrogation lasts for a couple of hours, then we are released. The girls have fallen asleep under the table.

We go to the house of my brother Ánde, who is living in Oslo. A couple of days later we fly to Leavdnja and are back in Sápmi.

It's not easy to come home. We have no money, no house, no car, no jobs. People stare at us, some seem to feel sorry for us. Few dare to talk to us apart from friends and drunkards. Journalists want to talk to us, but most of them call me a "bridge bomber." I find this odd, since I never bombed any bridge. Yet, the bridge we intended to bomb got a new name: "Somby Bridge."

Nils Kalliainen, a friend from Máttá-Várjjat, gives us an old green Mazda 818. We live in the basement of my parents' house in Sirbmá. One evening, we sit there eating spaghetti, when a policeman, Ove Samuelsen from Buolbmát, knocks on the door. He was my best childhood friend. Now he tells me that he has orders to arrest me. I tell him that I cannot go to prison, and that I have a doctor's certificate to prove it. He looks at the certificate suspiciously and asks to use the phone. I tell him that our phone isn't working. Ove insists that I have to come with him and that I will have to stand trial in Hámmárfeasta next week. After some back and forth, he agrees to make a phone call from the village.

The authorities have appointed Per Larsen as my attorney. He is from Hámmárfeasta. In my opinion, he is the worst attorney I could get. He's not a bad lawyer, but he was a dedicated supporter of the government during the Áltá campaign. Since I'm not allowed to change my attorney, I decide not to go to trial. I didn't even have the opportunity to talk to Larsen and get prepared.

While Ove is in the village making the phone call, Dagny and I throw some clothes into a bag and bring the girls upstairs to Grandma. We leave the food on the table and decide to head for Finland, first Ohcejohka, then Anár. At the border at Ohcejohka, the immigration officers stop us. I am afraid that I'll be arrested, but they only search the car for contraband. When they can't find any, we are allowed to continue.

In Anár, we meet a friend who agrees to hide me until the date for the trial has passed. I follow him to his home in Rivdul, while Dagny drives back home.

Ove, the policeman, came back to our house five minutes after we had left. The media has a field day: "Somby escaped again!"

Once we're past the scheduled day for the Hámmárfeasta trial, Sulo Klemet Aikio drives me to Luleju on the Swedish side of Sápmi, where I take a flight to Stockholm. Then I continue to Oslo by train. I am on my way to Sophie Minde Hospital, where I'm scheduled to have an operation on my arm. It still needs treatment.

Norwegian high school students on the train recognize me from pictures they've seen in the papers. They know that I'm on the run. They call the police who board the train as soon as we've crossed into Norway and arrest me. Big news in the media again: "Somby has been captured!"

At least the police allow me to have my operation. When

I wake up from anesthesia, a nurse has a message for me that throws me for a loop: "Your friend John Reier Martinsen has been killed in an accident."

The first thing I think of is a Norwegian who recently threatened to run me over with his car. Is this what happened to John Reier? I soon get answers.

On February 1, 1986, John Reier and Hermann Hansen traveled with their dogsleds from Áltá to Kárášjohka in the dark. They were wearing headlamps, and the dogs had reflective tags on them. They kept a distance of about two hundred yards between the sleds. At Joatkajávrri, they saw a snowmobile heading toward them. John Reier, who was first, stopped and sat down on a snowdrift with his headlamp on, waiting for the snowmobile to pass. When the snowmobile reached John Reier, the driver suddenly swerved to the right and hit him. The driver then continued and tried to hit Hermann in the same manner. Hermann only survived by jumping to the side at the very last moment. Some of his dogs were killed. When Hermann reached John Reier, he was already dead, and so were five of his dogs. John Reier had died of multiple head injuries. The driver of the snowmobile continued all the way to Áltá at full speed.

The police took no pictures at the scene of the accident. In court, they blame the cold, saying that the low temperatures had damaged the film.

In 1987, a nineteen-year-old man is convicted of second-degree manslaughter in the death of John Reier Martinsen. He receives a very short prison term. According to the verdict, he had negligently caused harm while driving under the influence.

People attending the trial are flabbergasted by all of the crucial evidence not being considered. Many of John Reier's friends and comrades believe that this was no accident but a political murder.* John Reier died at a time when hatred against Sámi and all critics of development projects was strong.

Today, it is hard to understand what that time was like. Death threats were common. Just a few days before John Reier died, I was stopped on the streets of Oslo by a man from northern Norway who said: "Look, Somby on tour! Too bad I'm not in my car, otherwise I would have run you over, you evil bridge bomber!" I never took those threats very seriously, but after John Reier's death it was different.

Regarding my trial, the authorities agree to make compromises. They appoint a new defense attorney, Steinar Bondø, and move the trial from Hámmárfeasta to Romsa. Steinar gets a list of the appointed judges, and we are given the opportunity to remove a juror. Lawrence Pootlass, chief of the Nuxalk Nation, and Luisea Mandell, the Nuxalk Nation's lawyer, are also present during the trial. The authorities have decided on the verdict and sentence beforehand: five months in prison, the same sentence they had given John Reier. I have already served that time in remand.

Later, I hear that the person who served as the presiding juror in our trial was a member of the secret police. Steinar and I therefore appeal the sentence and turn to the Supreme Court. But the only outcome is that they threaten us with a prison sentence and serious fines if we make that information public. The secret police must be secret, they argue.

---

* John Reier Martinsen was a high-ranking member of the Workers' Communist Party (Arbeidernes Kommunistparti, AKP), a Maoist organization and predecessor of today's Red Party (Rødt).

24.

I get a call from one of my cousins. He asks me to pick him up at a bar in Ohcejohka. He often helps me chop wood, so I do him the favor.

When I get to the bar, my cousin is with a group of drunk men. He has promised them to arrange a ride home for all. One of them is the former head of the regional secret police, Trygve Eriksen. He retired while I was in Canada and became an alcoholic.

I drop off the men at their respective homes. Trygve is the last one remaining. I have promised to drive him to Lákšjohka, where he lives. He talks the way drunk people do and complains about his brother calling him an alcoholic, even though he doesn't really drink that much. "Every now and again, I have a little party!"

Eventually, Trygve says, "Your mother-in-law once was my neighbor in Leavdnja. Did you know that?" I tell him that this can't be true, as my mother-in-law has never lived in Leavdnja. Trygve looks at me puzzled: "Wait! Are you not Per Ove?"

I reply, "Thanks for making me so young, Trygve, but I'm not Per Ove."

Trygve takes a good look at me. "Oh Lord, my creator!" He opens the door of the car and tries to get out while I'm driving at full speed. I grab him by the shoulder and, luckily, get a good hold of him, because he's wearing a leather jacket. The car door closes due to the headwind. I stop. Trygve starts crying. "What are you going to do with me?" He is sobbing like a child.

"I'm driving you to Lákšjohka," I say.

"Are you going to humiliate me in Lákšjohka?" Who would have thought that I'd ever be in a position where I have to comfort the former head of the regional secret police?

"No, I have no intentions to hurt you," I say. Trygve keeps on crying.

"I was given the task of watching you, and then, you devil, you escaped, and I don't know until it's all over the news. And you're in Canada! What do you think my bosses said?! It's your damn fault that I've become an alcoholic!" Trygve is now weeping uncontrollably. I do my best to calm him down. Eventually, we are able to continue. When we arrive at his home, I tell him to go to bed and sleep in peace. Several times, I need to assure him that I don't hate him. In the end, he shakes my hand the way drunk people do.

25.

Working as a journalist for the weekly newspaper *Sámi Áigi*, I am able to attend the opening session of the Sámi Parliament in October 1989. King Olav V is the master of ceremony. Numerous people in fancy clothes are waiting for him at the Kárášjohka Cultural Center. When he arrives, children hand him colorful bouquets of flowers. Then the king walks the red carpet, together with Kárášjohka's mayor Kjell Sæther, and Ole Henrik Magga, who has been elected as the first president of the Sámi Parliament.

Important (or self-important) Sámi politicians give speeches welcoming the king and the first members of the parliament. They thank the Norwegian government for its generosity in establishing the parliament. I'm not sure where these people have spent their lives. No one says a word about how the Sámi Parliament came only at considerable cost.

Eventually, one of the hunger strikers from 1979, Synnøve Persen, gets to speak. She is now the head of the Sami Artists' Union. Synnøve reads a poem, and she is the only person who dares to point out that the parliament is a result of the Álta protests. Then the Sámi Parliament is declared open.

I realize that I'm still a gullible child. I was disappointed to find out that the political parties of Norway were sending delegates to the parliament. I thought that a Sámi Parliament would represent our own organizations. But the only Sámi organization represented in the parliament is the Norwegian Sámi Association, whose very name implies submission to the Norwegian state.*

I go to many of the first Sámi Parliament sessions and listen to the discussions in the plenary. It is disheartening to see how many of them concern conflicts between the political parties of Norway. It's as if we are listening to debates on Norwegian Radio during a national election campaign. Everyone is trying to drag the others down.

After the plenary meetings, the members of parliament gather in a hotel to drink. There is no difference between a member of parliament being drunk and an ordinary fellow being drunk. Some of the politicians still haven't sobered up when they return to the plenary sessions the next day. There is a popular member of parliament from my area whom I'd considered the best Sámi politician. Now I am ashamed that I gave him my vote.

Eventually, the drinking in the hotel gets so out of hand that the members of parliament get an official warning. What do they do? They drink in their rooms instead and no longer show up drunk to the plenary sessions the next day; they don't show up at all.

What has the Sámi Parliament brought us? Foremost, Sámi bureaucracy, well-paid jobs, and a thriving industry around them. One can also argue that it strengthens Sámi society by virtue of, well, being the Sámi Parliament. But in terms of Sámi control over land and water, there has been no progress at all. On the contrary, things have probably gotten worse. The Sámi Parliament has long been working

---

* Norske Samers Riksforbund/Norgga Sámiid Riikasearvi (NSR) was founded in 1968 as an umbrella organization for local Sámi associations.

to establish the Finnmark Estate.* But does the Finnmark
Estate benefit the rights of the Sámi?

---

*   The Finnmark Estate (Finnmarkseiendommen/Finnmárkkuopmodat) is
     meant to administer the land of Finnmark, Norway's northernmost province
     with a sizeable Sámi community, on behalf of the province's population.
     Its board consists of three members appointed by the Sámi Parliament and
     three members appointed by the Finnmark County Council.

26.

The Finnmark Estate is an outcome of the Sámi Rights Committee. The politicians appointed to the Sámi Rights Committee were opposed to legal rights being tied to ethnicity. They insisted that, in Norway, everyone should have the same rights. As a result, the politicians (both Norwegian and Sámi) supported the idea that the Norwegian government, which had recently established the state-owned timber company Statskog, should hand over the administration of the land and water in Finnmark to a new institution. This institution was meant to be controlled by both the government of Finnmark and the Sámi Parliament. The Norwegian government figured that this would solve the problem of Norway's lack of Indigenous control over Sápmi's land and water. Indigenous people control 50 percent of the Finnmark Estate, but does this really make a difference? The only real difference is that now there is a fee for getting wood from the forest. Once upon a time, this was recognized as a human right.

In Canada, Indigenous people have the right to hunt moose without paying. In Sápmi, you can't hunt moose if you don't pay. You must both apply for a hunting license and get a permit for the area you want to hunt in. And when you kill a moose, you have to pay a certain amount per kilo. It's cheaper for me to buy moose meat in Gárasavvon on the Swedish side of Sápmi than to go hunting myself.

The Finnmark Estate also manages all inland fishing, except on the Deatnu River. There, one of the Norwegian kings once granted fishing rights to the local farmers, provided that they live there permanently, own property, and produce at least two thousand kilos of hay per year.

Comparing the land and water rights of the Sámi to those of other Indigenous peoples, it's easy to conclude that Sámi politicians have been tricked. As a Finnmark Estate board member or a Sámi Parliament delegate, you can certainly get travel expenses and financial compensation for meetings and the like, but it's not clear what the Sámi people get.

27.

In 2001, Arthur Manuel comes to visit his half brother, Ara, in Ohcejohka. We meet at the home of Márjjá Sofe, Ara's mother. Arthur has a young lawyer with him by the name of Nicole Schabus. When Arthur asks me why I haven't come to visit him in Canada, I remind him that my family is banned from Canada for life. Nicole smiles and says that a travel ban to Canada hardly ever lasts for life. She promises to investigate the matter upon her return.

A couple of months later, she calls me and says that the ban has been lifted. We are free to visit Canada whenever we want. In fact, Nicole has already applied for travel funds and a daily allowance from the Canadian government, which has been granted. Dagny is working at the post office and can't leave, but Márjjá Sofe, her son Ara, and I make our way to Canada.

It feels like coming home. In Vancouver, many friends are waiting at the airport. Some I have not seen in twenty years, some hadn't even been born when I was there. Sadly, the two most important people, Philip Paul and Georg Manuel, have passed away. I visit their graves with a heavy heart.

On the grave of George Manuel, there is a large tombstone. On the grave of Philip Paul, there is nothing. I'm told that there once was a wooden plaque, but it has withered away. According to Philip's sons it was their father's wish that the plaque would not be replaced with a more permanent one.

Brentwood Bay has changed. On Philip's land, there are now plenty of houses. But close to his home, there are only two new houses, one for each son. The sweat lodge and the longhouse I stayed in still look the same. I lie down in the loft of the longhouse, where I used to sleep. My mind recalls the spiritual conversations I had with Philip. Later, Philip's father-in-law, John Eliot, arrives, and we gather in the longhouse to commemorate Philip and his wife Fran, who has also passed away.

It is both wonderful and odd to see people who were children when I met them having grown into young adults. Some already have children of their own. I have maintained contact with them, and social media has made it even easier to stay in touch.

In Vancouver, they ask me to join a longhouse ceremony. I expect the same kind of ceremony we used to have with Philip, with a maximum of ten people. On the day of the ceremony, I see that they have built a new, large longhouse on the reserve. The reserve itself has been engulfed by the city. There are lots of people at the longhouse, more than a hundred it seems: children, teenagers, adults, and elderly people. Some of them are whites.

Inside the longhouse, there are three fires. It appears that we will have three separate groups during the ceremony. I am surprised to see people shouting, crying, and shaking already. Drummers have gathered around a man who is jumping up and down as if in a trance. They beat the drums until the man has calmed down. I ask a friend what is happening, and he says that, during the ceremony, people are freed from bad spirits and bitter thoughts. He explains that whites have a similar ceremony, even if they don't really understand what is happening when they shoot all those rockets in the sky on New Year's Eve.

It is uplifting to see that the spirituality Philip told me about has apparently become a natural part of life. But it also reminds me of how afraid the Sámi still are of their own spirituality, and how the Norwegians have succeeded in turning them into Sunday school children. The Norwegians stole our drums, and most of our people no longer know anything about them.*

Yes, the Sámi have started to yoik again. But it's usually reminiscent of a concert put on by Norwegians. The audience sits still, like in church, and the yoikers yoik. When the yoik is finished, the yoiker either bows (if a man) or curtsies (if a woman), the way they were taught by Norwegians. Meanwhile, the people in the audience politely applaud, and then they leave. In the longhouse, there are no yoiking stars. Everyone is yoiking and dancing. In moments like these I wonder whether we Sámi should really call ourselves Indigenous people.

We move on to Bella Coola to another ceremony. All the villagers are there. Lawrence Pootlass, who has since passed away, presides over the ceremony. There is dancing, singing, talking, and plenty of great food. Everything is free. I get a new name, Yaki, since I have now reached a mature age. The youngsters listen carefully when Lawrence tells them how his people adopted me and my family as their own. It is special to be back here after twenty years, and I'm moved that so many people have come together, among them many new members of the community. I'm glad that I'm able to thank the Nuxalk people.

Later, we stop at Alvin's place in Mount Currie. I am supposed to meet the spiritual healer, but we learn that he

---

* The Sámi drum (*goavddis*) plays a central role in traditional Sámi spirituality and culture. During Christianization, Sámi drums were systematically confiscated and destroyed.

Dressed up for a photo shoot.

passed away the day before. People have gathered at his home, where they are singing and beating drums. They continue until the day of the funeral. His body is taken to the sports hall, where a ceremony is held. Many people gather, locals as well as visitors from afar, as he was a highly respected man.

When Alvin and I arrive at the ceremony, plenty of people are outside. They say that one of the healer's family members has asked a priest to come, and that these people are waiting for the priest to leave. After some time, he does, accompanied by a small of group of men. Now, everyone goes inside.

The healer's body lies on a table on the stage. A group of people are dancing around it. They seem surprisingly upbeat, I almost get disco vibes. The people closest to the table are beating the drums. Two long queues have formed. One is to see the body. Before people come close, they are purified by smoke. The second queue is for a microphone. People can use it to say something about the healer and address his family. Because of all the drumming and singing, the people speaking in the microphone can hardly be heard, yet everyone gets to pay their respects.

I cannot stay until the end of the ceremony. I have a flight back to Sápmi the next day and need to catch a ride to Vancouver. In the car, I can't help comparing what I've just seen to Sámi funerals. At Sámi funerals, everyone sits quietly with their heads bowed. The priest is in full control and uses the sermon to instill Christian fear in everyone. All the Sámi get to do is carry the coffin to the grave, probably because it's hard work.

28.

In 2002, I receive a letter from the Sámi Parliament. They are inviting me to accept an honorary award along with everyone else who was involved in the hunger strike of 1979. The press reports that the Sámi Parliament is honoring a terrorist.

I understand that it's going to cause a headache for the Sámi Parliament, but I'm traveling to the ceremony, nonetheless. Most of the other hunger strikers are also there. Some have gone through hard times, two have passed away. Mihkkal Ánde has suffered a heart attack and Helene Margrete Olsen has died in a car accident. One of us was wise enough to refuse the award. Norway's TV2 and several other media outlets are present.

Mihkkal Eira, who came to visit me in Sirbmá before the award ceremony, passes away two years later. His funeral fills me with sorrow. Everyone praises his courage and the good work he has done for the Sámi community. That is nice to hear. But I know how Mihkkal and other hunger strikers have been treated by Sámi society. Sámi politicians and other public figures have put a blanket of silence over the events and taken credit themselves for the concessions that the Norwegian state has made to the Sámi since.

What have these concessions led to? We wanted to see respect for our rights and opportunities for future generations. None of this was to be traded on the altar of diplomacy. We knew that if you entered negotiations with the Norwegian state, you'd be awarded only by sacrificing your heritage. Future generations with no control over the land, their communities, and their Sámi identity won't have any opportunities.

The fight for Sámi rights is far from over. It will never be over. It is our responsibility, as Sámi and Indigenous people, to be the guardians of our land and our culture.

The awards handed out by the Sámi Parliament in 2002 had consequences for me. I was publicly denounced as a bridge bomber and terrorist, even by some Sámi Parliament members. I asked the parliament leaders to come out in support. They never did. People who claim to respect the legal system were outraged over the sentence I had received because they thought it was way too lenient. After all, I had tried to destroy public property! At least I'm satisfied with having done something that Norwegian society can't seem to get over. No one has been harmed in the action but myself. I have lost a hand and an eye, but I'm doing very well.

I don't know if there has been a change in Sámi politics, or if time simply makes a difference, but I feel it's become at least a little easier to be a former hunger striker. Bad conscience might be catching up with people who have looked down on us for a long time. I am trying to be generous with people who have vilified and excluded us. Maybe some of them find it easier to make peace with us while we're still alive. In that case, they don't have to do a turn-around when we die and suddenly praise and lift us up to the sky.

Let us honor the life and work of Mihkkal! Let us not destroy the future, even if some want to sit at the king's table and be important diplomats. Too many of the hunger strikers had to experience hardship, and not all of them found their way back to a society in which they weren't welcome.

There are still people who hate us for what we have done, particularly John Reier and me. That hatred is passed on from generation to generation. For these people, it seems easier to forget World War II.*

---

* Norway's occupation by Nazi Germany during World War II is a source of collective trauma.

29.

I am at the Riddu Riđđu Festival in 2012. Celebrities have grown older, children have grown up. During the festival's opening, Nils Magnus Tornensis and Ingá Juuso are introduced as guests of honor. Nils Magnus went on hunger strike for Sámi rights outside the Norwegian Parliament in 1981. Iŋgá has kept the yoik alive.

When I speak to Nils Magnus at the festival the following day, it pains me to see how thin and weak he is. He says that he suffers from the same disease as two of the other hunger strikers, Mihkkal and Ánte. The price for starvation is heavy, and now his body is giving in.

We go to the festival's restaurant, where Nils Magnus orders *biđus*, traditional Sámi meat soup. Patiently, he has to explain to the staff that the festival organizers promised him free food. Finally, he receives his biđus in a large paper cup and comes to sit with me. "This is what we get for the hard life we've had since the hunger strike," he says. "No one understands it but the ones who were part of it."

We talk about the hunger strikers and their lives. It's not a pleasant conversation. I've recorded some of what Nils Magnus said and quote it here with his permission.

> Three people are already dead and buried, and the majority of the people who are still alive are doing quite badly. It hurts that the Sámi politicians have disregarded us and what we did. It was a cheap way

for them to get respect, power, and money.... This festival wouldn't exist if it wasn't for us.

Nils Magnus tells me that he's been trying to talk to members of the Sámi Parliament. Most of them wouldn't even listen. After much effort, he was granted a meeting with Egil Olli, the Sámi Parliament's president from 2007 to 2013. Nils Magnus explained to him what it was like to be ostracized from one's own community and unable to work.

I asked him if the Sámi Parliament could help us with pensions, so that the short time we still have left to live wouldn't be all too difficult. His reply was: "It's a difficult case, yes, very difficult."

> At the height of our struggle, it was like a war. You were for Sápmi or against it, and Norwegian leaders made it very clear—both by decisions made in parliament and repression against us on the street—that they didn't think the Sámi had any rights to their land. If you compare us to people who fought in the Norwegian resistance against the Nazis, you will conclude that while those people were respected by Norwegian society, we were not respected by Sámi society. Many Sámi felt ashamed that we protested against the Norwegian state, although it was trying to eradicate Sámi rights and Sámi identity. Norwegians did not turn against Norwegian resistance fighters even if they killed their own people when they suspected them to be Nazi collaborators.

Despite his disappointment with the Sámi Parliament, Nils Magnus thinks that the Sámi Parliament is the most tangible outcome of our efforts. We have no other institution to turn to. "You cannot reject your own child," he says with a smile.

He proceeds to show me the response he wrote to the NSR when he was invited to one of their meetings as a guest of honor. I cite the response here with his permission.

> I don't want to feel bitter about the NSR or the Sámi Parliament. The NSR has led to the establishment of the Sámi Parliament and played a leading role in it until the Norwegians parties made their entry.
>
> I don't need to be modest, so let me be clear: The Sámi Parliament, and Sámi politics today, are the result of our activist work. That makes me a kind of parent to the Sámi Parliament and to contemporary Sámi politics. Therefore, I have a responsibility to say a few things about the relationship between us activists and the Sámi politicians.
>
> The Norwegian authorities eased the harsh policies of Norwegianization because of activists going on hunger strike. But the Sámi were told that it was the result of clever diplomacy by Sámi politicians.
>
> The king of Norway came to open the first session of the Sámi Parliament, and all of Sápmi's important people were there. But where were the activists? None of us had received an invitation. Did the Sámi politicians forget about us? Or had they agreed with the Norwegian state to forget about us? I don't know.
>
> I have thought a lot about how we have arrived at the current situation. Why do the leading politicians in Sápmi never mention us, even decades later? Why are they hiding the truth about what has changed Sápmi? I understand that there was a time when it was probably most convenient for Sámi politicians to

make everyone believe that they were the ones who had persuaded the Norwegian government to grant us our own parliament. But today?

Yet I notice some change. Since the turn of the millennium, more and more Sámi admit that there wouldn't be a Sámi Parliament without the hunger strikes. It became difficult to deny it, because an increasing number of social scientists and others who study history declared that this was the case. Had we not taken to action, Sápmi would still be under total Norwegian control.

So why did the relationship between the activists and the politicians in Sápmi turn sour? When we were active, we were an embarrassment to the politicians. They claimed that there was no need to take action. Today, they have to admit that our actions brought results, but they only do so grudgingly. As quickly as possible, they talk about something else. It's as if it were still dangerous to mention us in Sápmi. The NSR clearly bears responsibility for the activists being disregarded and ostracized. During the Álta campaign, all Sámi politicians were in the NSR. The Norwegian political parties played no role in Sámi politics before the establishment of the Sámi Parliament.

It often appears as if Sámi politicians are waiting for the activists to die and disappear. All of us. This will make it possible to forever hide the truth that it was not parliamentarians and diplomats who put an end to Norway's assimilation policies but rather activists.

Since everything has gone off course, it's not surprising that we are getting further from the truth with every year. Sámi politicians in Norway often present themselves as exemplary representatives of Indigenous people. They tell everyone about the huge difference that parliamentarism and diplomacy have made with respect to the Sámi. But what if someone told other Indigenous peoples the whole story? They would certainly ask about the lives of the activists, assuming that they are highly respected people among their own. Had that been the case, it would have been near impossible for the Sámi politicians to ignore us. Instead, some of us are already in the grave, and others are struggling.

Today, I feel that those who are on my side are fully on my side, and those who are against me are fully against me. At least, their attacks never stop. While I was at the Riddu Riđđu Festival this year as a guest of honor, someone broke three of my fingers. But not everyone treats me badly, not everyone thinks I'm crazy, and not everyone yells at me when they see me. Sometimes, I'm approached and hugged by people who are eighty years of age or older. "We must thank you," they say. "Without you, Sámi society would have never gained respect."

Wherever I go, the discussion quickly turns to the Sámi Parliament and Sámi politics. Quite often, people would say that the Sámi Parliament gives money to everyone except those who deserve it the most, the activists.

I grew up among reindeer herders. But our reindeer district was taken over by the Norwegian state, and we were left with nothing.* Today, I'm no longer

---

* Only Sámi are allowed to own reindeer in Norway, but the herding is strictly controlled by government authorities.

an asset to reindeer-herding communities since I no longer belong to a reindeer-herding district and hence have no reindeer. But I'm not good enough for other parts of Sámi society either, because I'm not an academic. So, even though I clearly see myself as a Sámi, there is no place for me in Sámi society. And in Norwegian society, I will be a protester and hunger striker as long as I live.

My life is precarious, no matter how you spin it. The worst was returning home to Guovdageaidnu after the hunger strike. I was yelled at and threatened, more than ever in my life. It was so devastating that I do not wish the same even for my biggest enemies. Imagine walking around in constant fear! It is not easy to survive when you are shunned by your own people.

Sure, the NSR can claim that they put on an event to honor us. But we know what kind of event that was. Some of us also know how it came about.

I once asked someone who had been working for the Sámi Parliament on public health issues if they had ever heard a Sámi politician ask what life was like for the activists, or whether they'd need some support. The person said that they had never heard a Sámi politician raise any such issue. I asked another person with the same job the same question, and I got the same answer. Naturally, it raises the question of who benefits from disavowing the Sámi activists. Have the political parties agreed to do this? How can we turn to the Sámi Parliament for help when we are not considered to be part of Sámi society?

I don't know whether some agreement has been made between the political parties that we must be ignored and shall not receive help from the Sámi Parliament. But, as I already pointed out, if we don't belong to Sámi society, you can't help us as Sámi.

We have not been able to work and earn money, and therefore we don't have a pension either. It feels like there is an invisible fence between the Sámi politicians and us. I can clearly see the fence, and so do the politicians. Every new Sámi politician learns about it.

Had we received the modest support that we pleaded and begged for, we would not have suffered the hardships we have suffered. It is difficult to explain to people what kind of life we have had. You need to experience it yourself before you can understand. It is no little thing when you realize that you no longer fit in with your own people.

It seems clear to me that my actions have contributed to a better life for the people in the north of Norway, and not just the Sámi! Why do Sámi politicians deny this? It leaves me puzzled. Now, I no longer have much time to wait for an explanation. My time is coming to an end.

It pains me that I might feel bitter over Sámi politics and Sámi politicians when it's time to leave this world. It would leave an ugly mark on Sámi society. I have risked my life in order to change things in Sápmi, and I should not have to die feeling bitter about the NSR or the Sámi Parliament; I should not die seeing Sámi politicians and Sámi society as enemies. It would be as if you were no longer speaking to your child. But the child doesn't recognize me as their father. Or I don't recognize them as my child. This is how I feel, and I don't know how else to look at it, even if I wish that we could tear down the invisible fence between us and reach common understanding.

No matter my feelings toward the NSR and the Sámi Parliament, I have never spoken ill of them, although I know that there are a lot of people who would be happy if I did.

Not only for me but also for the activist friends who are still alive, I demand the following, as respectfully as I can:

Give the activists the recognition they deserve!

Allow us to be part of Sámi society as the human beings we are!

Do not feel ashamed of us!

Do no longer hide the truth about Sámi politics!

Nils Magnus Tornensis

A few hours after talking to me, Nils Magnus is attacked by a man in a bar. His hand is seriously injured.

I'm often asked if I feel it was worth to sacrifice my hand and my ear for the cause. Well, there is no victory in losing a hand or an eye. But what good would it do for me or anyone else if I complained about it for the rest of my life? Life doesn't always turn out the way you expect it to or wish for. I have to consider all the good things that the accident has brought with it. I have met wonderful people whom I would never have met otherwise and who have given me a lot. I have learned who my real friends are. Think of the wind: it carries everything away that's weak and light, leaving only what's strong and heavy. I was left with the people who could go against the grain. Of course, it hurts when people you have trusted and counted on, including

THIRTY YEARS LATER

Before the famous Álta campaign, we had four *stállu* in Sápmi, in form of the colonial states of Norway, Sweden, Finland, and Russia.* They divided up Sápmi among themselves. With colonization being institutionalized, the Norwegian stállu turned into one with three heads: The first one looks like a Sámi and wears traditional clothing at least twice a year, on the Norwegian national day and on the Sámi national day; it is represented by the Sámi Parliament whose members we elect. The second is the Finnmark Estate, which the Sámi Parliament appoints two members to. The third is the Finnmark Commission, and especially its court that turns into law what the commission proposes.**

The members of the Sámi Parliament are elected every four years. The parliament elections are a big event in Sámi society. The Sámi Parliament has a president and is led by a council. It offers jobs and brings together people with much expertise. It is the single biggest workplace in Sápmi. But the Sámi Parliament has no political power. It has only consultation rights, and the Norwegian government can ignore whatever it says.

The members of the Sámi Parliament have always accepted this situation and seem proud of their consultation

---

* In Sámi mythology, *stállu* are mean-spirited giants.

** The Finnmark Commission (Finnmarkskommisjonen/Finnmárko-komišuvdna) is a legal body investigating the rights of use and ownership of the land in Finnmark.

people you were close to, get blown away. But, crucially, I am not alone! I am sober, I don't smoke, and I have always had strong friends around me, even when I was weak. They have never rejected me and helped me withstand the strongest of winds.

rights. The Norwegian government is certainly happy. Granting consultation rights to the Sámi Parliament and receiving its members to discuss matters concerning Sápmi satisfies international conventions on Indigenous peoples. But the relationship of power is clear: it is the Norwegian politicians who decide, not the Sámi ones.

The Sámi Parliament gets money from the Norwegian state. A lot. Some Norwegians, especially along the coast, are envious of the Sámi, thinking they get too much money. What they—or anyone else, for that matter—do not appreciate is that this money is coming from Sápmi; the Sámi not only pay taxes but plenty of administrative fees.

As I write this in 2016, we are witnessing the process of institutionalized colonialism first-hand. The latest news is that the entire Várjjat peninsula in eastern Finnmark has been recognized as part of the Finnmark Estate.* The Sea Sámi who left the area in the 1970s have lost all of their rights to the land as a consequence. The reindeer-herding Sámi of the area have lost their rights long ago.

The entire debate around land ownership is crazy. Like other Indigenous peoples, the Sámi didn't know any such thing as land ownership. By living in a certain area and using the land, you had the obligation to take care of it. People are guardians of nature, not owners. The lakes and the rivers were never emptied of fish because people understood what it meant to be a guardian; they were emptied of fish later, because fish were seen as a commodity. The Sámi always followed the spirits of nature.

The concept of landownership was introduced to Sápmi by colonizers. It means that whenever a Sámi community

---

* More examples could have been added after 2016. The overall pattern has not changed. It remains very difficult for Sámi communities to claim land ownership through the Finnmark Estate.

can't produce documents proving that they owed something, their land becomes the property of the Finnmark Estate. This is very convenient for the Norwegian state, because it makes land claims by Sámi communities near impossible.

It is mind-boggling to see the guru of Sámi politics smile on television while the Finnmark Commission, to which he belongs, is abolishing Sámi rights. The same man plays a central role in the new stállu, because he was also the leader of the NSR during the hunger strike and the first president of the Sámi Parliament.* I wonder about the salary that this man has received from the state for all his diplomatic efforts. It might be a cut above his actual achievements for Sápmi.

---

* A reference to Ole Henrik Magga.

ABOUT THE CONTRIBUTORS

Niillas Somby (born 1948) has been a prominent figure in the Sámi resistance against colonization since the 1970s. He was severely injured in an ill-fated 1982 sabotage action and subsequently found refuge among First Nations in Canada. He has worked as a reindeer herder, sailor, mechanic, photographer, and journalist. Today, he lives in Deanušaldi, on the Norwegian side of Sápmi.

Gabriel Kuhn is an Austrian-born writer and translator living in Sweden. Among his book publications are *Turning Money into Rebellion: The Unlikely Story of Denmark's Revolutionary Bank Robbers* and *Liberating Sápmi: Indigenous Resistance in Europe's Far North*.

ABOUT PM PRESS

PM Press is an independent, radical publisher of critically necessary books for our tumultuous times. Our aim is to deliver bold political ideas and vital stories to all walks of life and arm the dreamers to demand the impossible. Founded in 2007 by a small group of people with decades of publishing, media, and organizing experience, we have sold millions of copies of our books, most often one at a time, face to face. We're old enough to know what we're doing and young enough to know what's at stake. Join us to create a better world.

PM Press
PO Box 23912
Oakland, CA 94623
www.pmpress.org

PM Press in Europe
europe@pmpress.org
www.pmpress.org.uk

FRIENDS OF PM PRESS

These are indisputably momentous times—the financial system is melting down globally and the Empire is stumbling. Now more than ever there is a vital need for radical ideas.

In the many years since its founding—and on a mere shoestring—PM Press has risen to the formidable challenge of publishing and distributing knowledge and entertainment for the struggles ahead. With hundreds of releases to date, we have published an impressive and stimulating array of literature, art, music, politics, and culture. Using every available medium, we've succeeded in connecting those hungry for ideas and information to those putting them into practice.

Friends of PM allows you to directly help impact, amplify, and revitalize the discourse and actions of radical writers, filmmakers, and artists. It provides us with a stable foundation from which we can build upon our early successes and provides a much-needed subsidy for the materials that can't necessarily pay their own way. You can help make that happen—and receive every new title automatically delivered to your door once a month—by joining as a Friend of PM Press. And, we'll throw in a free T-shirt when you sign up.

Here are your options:

- **$30 a month** Get all books and pamphlets plus a 50% discount on all webstore purchases

- **$40 a month** Get all PM Press releases (including CDs and DVDs) plus a 50% discount on all webstore purchases

- **$100 a month** Superstar—Everything plus PM merchandise, free downloads, and a 50% discount on all webstore purchases

For those who can't afford $30 or more a month, we have **Sustainer Rates** at $15, $10 and $5. Sustainers get a free PM Press T-shirt and a 50% discount on all purchases from our website.

Your Visa or Mastercard will be billed once a month, until you tell us to stop. Or until our efforts succeed in bringing the revolution around. Or the financial meltdown of Capital makes plastic redundant. Whichever comes first.

Liberating Sápmi: Indigenous Resistance in Europe's Far North

Gabriel Kuhn

ISBN: 978-1-62963-712-9
$17.00   220 pages

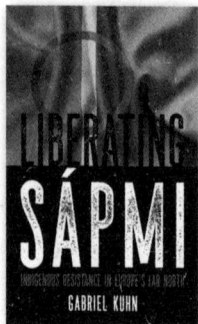

The Sámi, who have inhabited Europe's far north for thousands of years, are often referred to as the continent's "forgotten people." With Sápmi, their traditional homeland, divided between four nation-states—Norway, Sweden, Finland, and Russia—the Sámi have experienced the profound oppression and discrimination that characterize the fate of indigenous people worldwide: their lands have been confiscated, their beliefs and values attacked, their communities and families torn apart. Yet the Sámi have shown incredible resilience, defending their identity and their territories and retaining an important social and ecological voice—even if many, progressives and leftists included, refuse to listen.

Liberating Sápmi is a stunning journey through Sápmi and includes in-depth interviews with Sámi artists, activists, and scholars boldly standing up for the rights of their people. In this beautifully illustrated work, Gabriel Kuhn, author of over a dozen books and our most fascinating interpreter of global social justice movements, aims to raise awareness of the ongoing fight of the Sámi for justice and self-determination. The first accessible English-language introduction to the history of the Sámi people and the first account that focuses on their political resistance, this provocative work gives irrefutable evidence of the important role the Sámi play in the resistance of indigenous people against an economic and political system whose power to destroy all life on earth has reached a scale unprecedented in the history of humanity.

The book contains interviews with Mari Boine, Harald Gaski, Ann-Kristin Håkansson, Aslak Holmberg, Maxida Märak, Stefan Mikaelsson, May-Britt Öhman, Synnøve Persen, Øyvind Ravna, Niillas Somby, Anders Sunna, and Suvi West.

"I'm highly recommending Gabriel Kuhn's book Liberating Sápmi *to anyone seeking to understand the world of today through indigenous eyes. Kuhn concisely and dramatically opens our eyes to little-known Sápmi history, then in the perfect follow-up brings us up to date with a unique collection of interviews with a dozen of today's most brilliant contemporary Sámi voices. Bravo."*
—Buffy Sainte-Marie, Cree, singer-songwriter

Turning Money into Rebellion: The Unlikely Story of Denmark's Revolutionary Bank Robbers

Edited by Gabriel Kuhn

ISBN: 978-1-60486-316-1
$19.95   240 pages

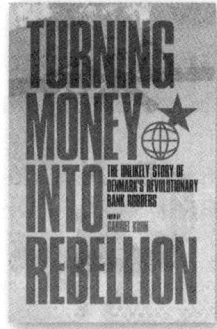

Blekingegade is a quiet Copenhagen street. It is also where, in May 1989, the police discovered an apartment that had served Denmark's most notorious twentieth-century bank robbers as a hideaway for years. The Blekingegade Group members belonged to a communist organization and lived modest lives in the Danish capital. Over a period of almost two decades, they sent millions of dollars acquired in spectacular heists to Third World liberation movements, in particular the Popular Front for the Liberation of Palestine (PFLP). In May 1991, seven of them were convicted and went to prison.

The story of the Blekingegade Group is one of the most puzzling and captivating chapters from the European anti-imperialist milieu of the 1970s and '80s. *Turning Money into Rebellion: The Unlikely Story of Denmark's Revolutionary Bank Robbers* is the first-ever account of the story in English, covering a fascinating journey from anti-war demonstrations in the late 1960s via travels to Middle Eastern capitals and African refugee camps to the group's fateful last robbery that earned them a record haul and left a police officer dead.

The book includes historical documents, illustrations, and an exclusive interview with Torkil Lauesen and Jan Weimann, two of the group's longest-standing members. It is a compelling tale of turning radical theory into action and concerns analysis and strategy as much as morality and political practice. Perhaps most importantly, it revolves around the cardinal question of revolutionary politics: What to do, and how to do it?

"This book is a fascinating and bracing account of how a group of communists in Denmark sought to aid the peoples of the Third World in their struggles against imperialism and the dire poverty that comes with it. The book contains many valuable lessons as to the practicalities of effective international solidarity, but just as importantly, it is a testament to the intellectual courage of the Blekingegade Group."
—Zak Cope, author of *Dimensions of Prejudice: Towards a Political Economy of Bigotry*

The Mohawk Warrior Society: A Handbook on Sovereignty and Survival

Louis Karoniaktajeh Hall

Edited by Kahentinetha Rotiskarewake, Philippe Blouin, Matt Peterson, and Malek Rasamny

ISBN: 978-1-62963-941-3
$27.95   320 pages

The first collection of its kind, this anthology by members of the Mohawk Warrior Society uncovers a hidden history and paints a bold portrait of the spectacular experience of Kanien'kehá:ka survival and self-defense. Providing extensive documentation, context, and analysis, the book features foundational writings by prolific visual artist and polemicist Louis Karoniaktajeh Hall (1918–1993)—such as his landmark 1979 pamphlet *The Warrior's Handbook*, as well as selections of his pioneering artwork. This book contains new oral history by key figures of the Rotisken'rhakéhte's revival in the 1970s and tells the story of the Warriors' famous flag, their armed occupation of Ganienkeh in 1974, and the role of their constitution, the Great Peace, in guiding their commitment to freedom and independence. We hear directly the story of how the Kanien'kehá:ka Longhouse became one the most militant resistance groups in North America, gaining international attention with the Oka Crisis of 1990. This autohistory of the Rotisken'rhakéhte is complemented by a Mohawk history timeline from colonization to the present, a glossary of Mohawk political philosophy, and a new map of Iroquoia in Mohawk language. At last, the Mohawk Warriors can tell their own story with their own voices, and to serve as an example and inspiration for future generations struggling against the environmental, cultural, and social devastation cast upon the modern world.

"This clear and stimulating book had me on edge from beginning to end. No matter who we are we can learn from these histories of the Iroquois Confederacy as related by its present-day members, lessons pertaining to nonhierarchical political organization and the care of the land. In the age of Black Lives Matter this work makes the case for autonomous life-spaces free of US or Canadian state control."
—Michael Taussig, Class of 1933 Professor of Anthropology, Columbia University